ENDLESS PATH

Ancient Egypt

This is a **FLAME TREE** book
First published in 2006

Publisher and Creative Director: Nick Wells
Designer: Lucy Robins
Project Editor: Catherine Emslie
Picture Researcher: Gemma Walters
Production: Kelly Fenlon, Chris Herbert and Claire Walker

Special thanks to: Rosanna Singler

FLAME TREE PUBLISHING
Crabtree Hall, Crabtree Lane
Fulham, London SW6 6TY
United Kingdom
www.flametreepublishing.com

06 08 10 09 07
1 3 5 7 9 10 8 6 4 2

Flame Tree is part of The Foundry Creative Media Company Limited

A copy of the CIP data for this book is available from the British Library.

ISBN-10: 1-84451-516-8
ISBN-13: 978-1-84451-516-5

As dates for the history of Ancient Egypt differ from source to source, the reader should be aware that the dates in this book have been made consistent with those used in the *British Museum Dictionary of Ancient Egypt* by Ian Shaw and Paul Nicholson. (Published for the Trustees of the British Museum by British Museum Press, 1995)

Printed in China

ENDLESS PATH

Ancient Egypt

Author: Brenda Ralph Lewis

Foreword: Dr Robert Morkot

FLAME TREE
PUBLISHING

Contents

Foreword

Egypt has fascinated and attracted outsiders since ancient times. The Greeks and Romans were astounded by its antiquity – and antiquities, by its bizarre animal-headed gods and the strange practice of mummification: indeed, all of the things that continue to beguile us today. It held the same fascination for the peoples and kingdoms of the ancient Near East too; but it was also seen at times as a threat. From the time when Egypt was united under one ruler – the 'pharaoh' – about 3000 BC, it was the most enduring, and seemingly unchanging, of all the kingdoms that arose in the region. Elsewhere, cities and kingdoms expanded their power for a time, but Egypt continued, and, until quite late in its history, was unconquered by outsiders. Of course, there were changes of dynasty, and periods of economic and political instability, but there was continuity.

Much of that continuity came through the ruler, the 'pharaoh'. The word derives from the Egyptian *per-aa*, or 'Great house' (palace). From the earliest times the prime role of the pharaoh was to ensure that the annual inundation o fthe River Nile was good. He was, therefore, the chief priest who interceded with the gods to maintain the order of the universe. He was also the chief administrator, judge and army leader, but it was the religious duties that the monuments emphasized above all others. Dynasties came and went, but the role of the king remained fundamentally the same for the enormous span of

Egyptian history. And, importantly, the image of the ruler remained essentially the same: the Roman emperors were depicted on Egyptian temple walls precisely as the first pharaohs had been depicted over three thousand years earlier.

Egypt was the first 'nation state'; with one ruler, one government, one language and culture. It was large, both in terms of area and of population, particularly compared with the small city-states of Syria and Palestine. It was also rich: both in food and in 'luxury' materials. Every year at midsummer, the Nile flooded, bringing with it the rich fertilizing silt from the Ethiopian mountains. This ensured that there were ample supplies of grain, provided, of course, that the inundation was good. There were times of poor floods, and times of famine, and this explains why Egypt developed in the way that it did: storage of grain for times of poor harvest led Egypt to develop one of the most complex administrations. The result was a highly centralized state: the state organized the land, the state stored the produce and distributed food as wages. The state also fed people and organized major projects, such as pyramid and temple-building, during the time when the agricultural land was under water. Those projects celebrated the state itself, in the form of the gods and the king.

These great monuments of Egypt were man-made mountains of stone. They were built to last. Stone was plentiful in the Nile Valley, but good timber was scarce. Monuments for the gods, and the dead who had joined them, were therefore built of limestone, sandstone and granite. The living used bricks from the Nile silt, a material that could be renewed regularly, and was cool in summer and warm in winter. The qualities of sawn stone, and the simple construction techniques available, therefore dictated the style of Egyptian monumental architecture: solid and square. But the surfaces provided plenty of space for images and writing. In temples, the gods appeared in all their many forms, with the pharaoh performing the rituals that ensured the stability of the universe. In tombs, the walls were covered with scenes of all aspects of Egypt's agricultural and artisan production, so that the tomb owner (a member of the ruling elite) could continue to enjoy them for eternity.

It is these tomb scenes that make Ancient Egypt seem so alive to us now. Much of what we see of the rural life can still be seen in the Egyptian countryside today. Although increasingly rare, there are still houses made of the traditional mud brick, and when viewed from the Nile, the ancient temples still dominate the landscape in places. In Egypt the past seems somehow accessible, and yet it still seems in many ways as mysterious, and as alluring, as it did to the Greeks and Romans two thousand years ago.

Dr Robert Morkot, 2006

Lecturer, Department of Archaeology, University of Exeter

Land of the Pharaohs: The History of Ancient Egypt

The Gift of the Nile

Herodotus (*c.* 485–425 BC), a Greek writer who travelled extensively in the Middle East and beyond, observed in his *Histories*: 'Egypt is the gift of the Nile.' It was true. Without the Nile, the world's longest river, Ancient Egypt would never have existed. Beyond the river and its environs, there was only bone-dry desert, infertile except for a few oases, burning hot by day, freezing cold by night. The Nile was the secret of life in Ancient Egypt, making possible the growth of its culture, language, literature, science, religious practices, mythology, art, architecture – everything, in fact, that went to create the first civilizations that appeared in ancient times. Above all, the Nile produced the fertile soil that sustained the Ancient Egyptians in a paradise of plenty. A proliferation of food – wheat, barley, vegetables, fruit, milk, meat – along the Nile Valley meant that even the poorest labourer did not go hungry.

The History of Ancient Egypt – a Problem

If history is a narrative of events, then it cannot really describe any contemporary account of Ancient Egypt. Although Herodotus' book describing his travels in the Middle East and beyond was entitled *Histories*, his coverage of Ancient Egypt dealt far more with culture and customs. Two centuries after Herodotus, Manetho, an Egyptian priest, wrote his *Aegyptiaca*, a history of Egypt. Unfortunately, Manetho's account, which he dedicated to the Pharaoh Ptolemy II (285–246 BC) was heavily laced with myths and folk tales, and, although he set a precedent for later historians by dividing the reigns of Egyptian rulers into 31 dynasties, he did not realise that many dynasties ruled at the same time during periods of upheaval. Ultimately, history had to wait until modern archaeologists arrived to excavate the tombs and other relics of the Nile civilization and from them piece together the 3,000-year old story of Ancient Egypt.

The Turin Kinglist and the Palermo Stone

The sometimes unsatisfactory raw material from which the history of Ancient Egypt had to be compiled was typified by the Turin Kinglist and the Palermo Stone. The Kinglist was written on a papyrus acquired in the 1820s by the French proconsul in Egypt, Bernardino Drovetti (1776–1852), and it later became the property of the Museo Egizio in Turin. It comprised the names of some 300 rulers up to the the reign of Pharaoh Ramesses II (1279–1213 BC), and the length of their reigns. Kings whose re sidence was in a certain city were grouped together.

The Palermo Stone, discovered in around 1866, was an inscribed piece of a basalt stele which also featured the names of ancient rulers. The stone, inscribed on both sides, went back a great deal further than the Turin Kinglist, to the days of the Fifth Dynasty (2494–2345 BC).

Jean-François Champollion and the Rosetta Stone

Jean-François Champollion (1790–1832) was the French linguist and scholar who discovered how to read Ancient Egyptian hieroglyphs. Champollion was something of a prodigy. He was still a student at the Lyceum in Grenoble when he published a paper on Ancient Egyptian language in 1807, aged 16. In 1822, he began work on translating the hieroglyphic inscriptions on the Rosetta Stone, a black granite stele discovered in 1799 in the western delta of Egypt. The stone contained a decree issued by the Pharaoh Ptolemy V, dated 196 BC, which was written in three scripts – Greek, Egyptian demotic and hieroglyphics. By 1824, Champollion was able to announce that he had deciphered the names of Ptolemy and Cleopatra and, most importantly, understood the phonetics and ideograms of the hieroglyphic system. This was the great breakthrough that made it possible for Egyptologists to read the ancient papyri and inscriptions on monuments, tombs, stele and stones.

Which Pharaoh?

Dates in The History of Ancient Egypt need to be taken as approximate, partly because there is no sure way of knowing precisely when an event occurred. Another factor is the disagreement between some Egyptologists who support differing theories. One classic dispute, still being aired, is over the identity of the pharaoh who featured in the Bible story of the Exodus of the Hebrews, led by Moses, from Egypt. Candidates include, among others, Thutmose III (1479–1425 BC), Amenhotep III (1390–1352 BC), Ramesses II (1279–1213 BC) – the most frequently cited – and Ramesses' son Merneptah I (1213–1203 BC). It has been claimed that due to a misreading of the Ancient Egyptian calendar, the Exodus and the pharaoh's identity have been shifted to a time up to two centuries later than their 'real' date.

Famous Pharaohs of Ancient Egypt

Hatshepsut (1473–1458 BC)

Hatshepsut was the most powerful and influential of Ancient Egyptian queens. When her marriage to her half-brother Thutmose II (1492–1479 BC) failed to produce a male heir, Hatshepsut took steps to gain control over her husband's successor, the son of one of his minor wives. After the boy, Thutmose III (1479–1425 BC), became pharaoh on the death of his father, Hatshepsut had herself proclaimed regent. Next, enlisting support from the priests of Amun, she had herself crowned king of Egypt. Though officially co-regent with the young Thutmose, Hatshepsut was, in effect, sole ruler. Hatshepsut's reign was marked by much temple- and other building, and several high-profile trading and military expeditions. Numerous monuments to Hatshepsut were erected, many of them showing the queen wearing a false royal beard. But mystery surrounds the end of her reign. It is not known whether Hatshepsut died a natural death or was forcibly removed from power.

Thutmose III (1479–1425 BC)

Thutmose III, who became pharaoh as a young boy, had to wait 21 years before he escaped the tutelage of his stepmother Hatshepsut and, in about 1458 BC, assumed full royal powers. Over the next 33 years or so, Thutmose became one of Egypt's greatest pharaohs. In *c.* 1457 BC, he personally led his army at the battle of Megiddo to put down a dangerous rebellion in Syria-Palestine. Subsequently, he fought 17 military campaigns to extend the borders of Egypt into Asia Minor and north-west Mesopotamia. His fleet controlled the eastern Mediterranean. At home, Thutmose enlarged the religious centre devoted to the god Amun and built numerous temples in the Nile Delta region and as far south as Nubia. However, it appears to have been relatively late in his reign before Thutmose took his revenge on the manipulative Hatshepsut by removing her name from her monuments and substituting his own.

Amenhotep IV (Akhenaten) (1352–1336 BC)

Amenhotep IV, who became pharaoh *c.* 1352 BC, wanted to return Egypt to the way it had been in the Old Kingdom, dominated by the cult of the visible Sun Disc, the 'Aten'. He built a temple to Aten at Karnak and a new capital, Akhetaten – 'horizon of Aten' – to displace Memphis and Thebes as prime religious and secular centres. The names of Amun and other Egyptian gods were erased from temple walls. In around 1347 BC, Amenhotep changed his name to Akhenaten – 'effective-spirit of the Sun Disc'. The new solar cult placed all emphasis on the pharaoh as the only channel between the god and people (see chapter five, page 224). It is impossible to know how this was received at the time, but following Akhenaten's death there was a swift return to a richer, polytheistic, religion in which the people could communicate directly with their gods. Akhenaten's name never appeared in the official king lists, and his town and temples were sytematically dismantled and the stone reused.

Tutankhamun (1336–1327 BC)

Tutankhamun, son and successor of Akhenaten, owes his fame entirely to the discovery of his untouched tomb in 1922 by the British archaeologist Howard Carter (1874–1939). Since his father promoted worship of the Sun god Aten above the state deity Amun, he was at first known as Tutankhaten, the living image of the Aten. Later, as perhaps his father's heresies had provoked a violent reaction, his name was changed to Tutankhamun. He was only about eight years old when his father died and he became pharaoh. During his short reign – Tutankhamen died when he was only about 18 years of age – Akhenaten's reforms were progressively undone. This included a move back to Memphis from the new capital of Akhetaten and the re-opening of the state-religion temples. Akhenaten's preference for natural, realistic art was replaced by the traditional formality it had supplanted.

Ramesses II (1279–1213 BC)

Ramesses II was pharaoh of Egypt for 67 years, a reign so lengthy that many of his heirs died before him; he was eventually succeeded by his thirteenth son, Merenptah I. Ramesses was responsible for building a mass of temples, monuments and statues and a new capital, Piramesse in the eastern Delta region. The Nubian temples cut into the rockface at Abu Simbel and still extant, were constructed during Ramesses' reign, together with the vast Ramesseum, his mortuary temple in western Thebes. The event most often celebrated on the walls of Ramesses' temples and on papyri – 13 full accounts in all – was his victory over the Hittites at the battle of Qadesh in *c.* 1274 BC. It was not an overwhelming triumph, and was followed by a treaty and Ramesses' political marriages with two Hittite princesses, but it served to control the threat the Hittites posed to the security of Egypt.

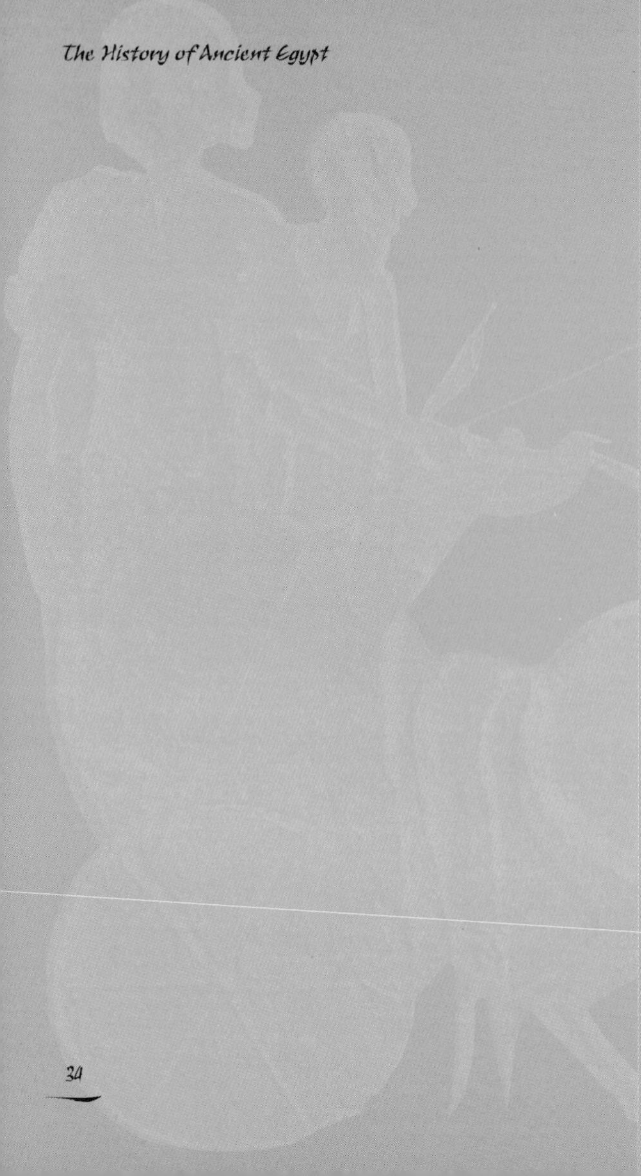

The Battle of Megiddo (c. 1457 BC)

In his graphic account (the earliest of such detail in history), the military scribe, Tjaneni, recounted how a 10,000-strong army, led by Pharaoh Thutmose III, marched into central Palestine and confronted rebels stirred up by the prince of Qadesh and Egypt's most powerful rivals, the Mitannians. The Qadeshi army had taken control of outposts along the Megiddo pass. But Thutmose, leading the way in his chariot, battered through to the valley beyond, where the rebels awaited him near Megiddo fortress. Thutmose led his northern wing in a determined assault, driving his forces between the rebel positions and the fortress. The defeated rebels managed to flee into Megiddo itself, however, resulting in a several-months-long siege of the city in order to secure victory.

The Archaeology of Ancient Egypt

Serious effort to uncover the secrets of Ancient Egyptian civilization is a relatively recent phenomenon. The pioneering work began a little over two centuries ago, in 1798, when French scholars arrived in Egypt with Napoleon's invading army. They were the first to systematically explore Egypt and record its flora and fauna as well as what could then be discovered of its history. Throughout the nineteenth century and into the twentieth, private expeditions, chiefly by European enthusiasts, uncovered Ancient Egyptian tombs, mummies, statues, stelae, monuments and artifacts. At first the focus was on finding the fabled treasure of the pharaohs, the feature of Tutankhamun's tomb, discovered in 1922 by Howard Carter, that excited most public interest. Later, though, the emphasis turned to the patient, if less glamorous fieldwork that could take years of digging, sorting, cleaning and preserving, before the immensely ancient world that once flourished by the Nile was revealed.

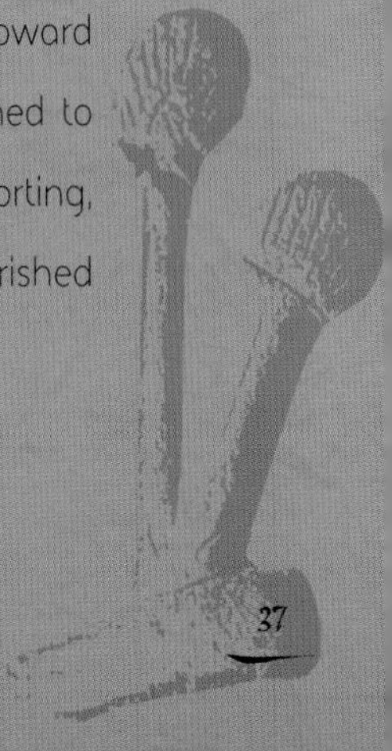

Valley of the Kings, Valley of the Queens

A major focus for archaeological digs in Egypt was the Valley of the Kings, which is sited on the west bank of the Nile about 5 km (3.1 miles) west of Luxor. It consists, in fact, of two valleys, the eastern of which was the main cemetery for rulers of the 18th, 19th and 20th dynasties, and the western, which contains four tombs. A total of 62 royal and private tombs exist in the two valley cemeteries, with those for pharaohs dating from Thutmose I (1504–1492 BC) to Ramesses XI (1099–1069 BC). The most famous tomb in the eastern valley, the tomb of Tutankhamun (1336–1327 BC), is the only *king's* tomb that was not completely plundered, although several other tombs in the Valley were found virtually intact. The Valley of the Queens contains 75 tombs in which the wives and sons of some New Kingdom rulers were buried.

Ancient Egyptian Chronology

Predynastic Period (5500–3100 BC)

Late Neolithic (New Stone) Age.
First agricultural settlements.

Early Dynastic Period (3100–2686 BC)

Dynasties 1 (to 2890 BC) and 2

Skilled craftsmanship; stone buildings; move from small settlements to larger communities in towns and cities.

By tradition, Menes is first ruler of FirstDynasty and said to have founded the Egyptian state and unified Upper and Lower Egypt. (However, since discovery of the Narmer Palette, first ruler generally believed to have been called Narmer – either one and same as Menes or his predecessor.)

The Old Kingdom (2686–2181 BC)

Dynasties 3, 4, 5 and 6

Third Dynasty (2686–2613 BC): First 'step' pyramids.

Fourth Dynasty (2613–2494 BC): Pyramids with smooth sloping sides introduced. Cult of Sun is established.

Fifth Dynasty (2494–2345 BC): Solar temples built, decorated with texts. *Pyramid Texts* recount the afterlife of the king.

Sixth Dynasty (2345–2181 BC): Old Kingdom in decline. King's power weakening in Nubia. Annual inundation of the Nile decreasing. Flood controls put in place to regulate flow of water.

First Intermediate Period

Dynasties 7, 8, 9, 10 and 11

Seventh and Eighth Dynasties (2181–2125 BC): Central government losing power, divisions within Egypt, a number of short reigns. Civil war.

Ninth and 10th Dynasties (2160–2025 BC): Mentuhotep II defeats kings of these dynasties and reunites Egypt.

Middle Kingdom (2055–1650 BC)

Dynasties 11, 12, 13 and 14

11th Dynasty (2055–1985 BC): Impressive monuments built in Egypt. Egyptian economy improves after chaos of First Intermediate Period. However, the throne may have been usurped from the last king of the 11th Dynasty, Mentuhotep IV (1992–1985 BC) whose name was omitted from later kinglists.

12th Dynasty (1985–1795 BC): Mentuhotep's vizier, Amenemhat I (1985–1955 BC) succeeds him, possibly by coup d'état. Administrative centre moved from Thebes to new city Itj-tawi (The One who Siezes the Two Lands). Thebes gains importance as focus of cult of Amun. Spoils won in military campaigns in Nubia finance new building programme. Fortresses built to keep out invading desert nomads. Control regained in region south of the First Nile Cataract. Senusret III (1874–1855 BC) strengthens central government, taking power away from disruptive local governors. Twelfth Dynasty declines after 1808 BC, trade in copper and turquoise from Sinai ceases. Foreign pharaohs take charge in Egypt.

13th and 14th Dynasties (1795–1650 BC): Throne is several times seized by non-royal usurpers. Famine in Nile Delta, spread of plagues in Egypt.

Second Intermediate Period (1650–1550 BC)

Dynasties 15, 16 and 17

Egypt open to foreign aggression. Canaanites, led by the 'Hyksos' ('Rulers of foreign lands') come to power in 1640 BC but cannot maintain control over the whole country. Even so, the Hyksos introduce use of horses and chariots in warfare.

Thebes regains independence, founding its own dynasty, by trading with the Hyksos. Thebans acquire military technology from the Hyksos – curved swords, body armour, helmets. Used to defeat the Hyksos and inaugurate the New Kingdom. Three dynasties contemporary with each other.

The New Kingdom (1550–1069 BC)

Dynasties 18 (to 1295 BC), 19 (to 1186 BC) and 20

Ahmose (1550–1525 BC) reunites Egypt (beginning of the 'New Kingdom') and introduces a new prosperity and security. Territory conquered by the rulers of the New Kingdom stretches from Syria-Palestine in the north to the Second Cataract of the Nile in Nubia in the south. Later conquests extend Egyptian territory to the River Euphrates in present-day Iraq. Egypt becomes most powerful nation in ancient Near East. Spoils of war finance temple-building, including great temple at Karnak in Thebes, dedicated to the god Amun.

Hostilities flare between Egypt and the Hittites but are ended by a peace treaty in *c.* 1258 BC. About 45 years of peace follow until around 1213 BC, when Pharaoh Ramesses II dies. Under his weak successors, the priests of Amun increase their political power in Upper Egypt. The Egyptian military also claim a share in government. Government breaks up into mutually hostile factions. End of the New Kingdom.

Third Intermediate Period (1069–747 BC)

Dynasties 21, 22, 23 and 24

Power divided between numerous kings with dynasties overlapping. Private wealth amassed, particularly by the priests. Civil war between rival rulers. Nubians take advantage of Egypt's subsequent weakness to invade and set up a dynasty of their own, the 25th.

Late Period (747–332 BC)

Dynasties 25 (to 656 BC), 26 (664–525 BC), 27 (to 404 BC), 28 (to 399 BC), 29 (to 380 BC) and 30 (to 343 BC)

The Nubians, having brought peace and stability to Egypt, are soon confronted with the cruel and bloodthirsty Assyrians, who have founded the first military empire and made themselves the terror of Mesopotamia. In *c.* 664 BC the Assyrians plunder Thebes and destroy temples and tombs. Egypt is ruled by pharaohs of the 26th Dynasty (from Sais in the Delta), who are initially Assyrian vassals, but bring peace and prosperity to the country.

The Saites are unseated in 525 BC by a Persian invasion. The Persians, in their turn, are thrown out in 404 BC by King Amyrtaios (404–399 BC). Egypt's regained independence lasts 60 years, until 343 BC when the Persians return to plunder temples, butcher people and animals and demand extortionate tributes from the survivors. The experience is so terrible that the Egyptians welcome the Macedonian conqueror Alexander the Great who liberates them from the Persians, but establishes his own foreign dynasty to rule over them.

After Alexander's Macedonian Dynasty (332–305 BC) the Ptolemaic pharaohs, descendants of Alexander's general Ptolemy Soter I, rule Egypt for 275 years (305–30 BC) before the Romans take over in 30 BC and turn Egypt into a province of their empire. Egypt would not be an independent country again for almost 2,000 years, until 1922.

The Last of the Seven Wonders: Architecture and Infrastructure

Architecture and Infrastructure

Awe-inspiring Architecture

The overriding impression of Ancient Egyptian architecture is one of enormous size and bulk – massive stone monuments, lofty pyramids, elaborate temple complexes. This prodigious image is somewhat deceptive. The pyramids, for example, were not built to accord with a particular architectural taste: the imperative was to provide a fitting environment for the pharaoh to make a safe journey to the afterlife. The use of stone has proved fortuitous. Ancient Egypt was much more a land of adobe mud brick, the material used for houses and even for royal palaces and fortresses. Mud-brick buildings were cool in summer and warm in winter, but were susceptible to the elements and had to be renewed on a regular basis. This is why most Ancient Egyptian towns have disappeared while the great stone monuments have survived for millennia since they were first constructed.

How Egyptian Monuments Were Constructed

The huge stone structures of Ancient Egypt were built by the post-and-lintel method, despite the development of the curved arch during the Fourth Dynasty of the New Kingdom (2613–1494 BC). In the post-and-lintel method, an opening, such as a doorway, was spanned by horizontal beams supported on posts or columns. Some stone buildings had flat roofs made of big stone blocks that were held up by external walls and columns placed close together. The thick walls characteristic of large buildings, particularly the pyramid tombs, had just a few narrow openings which helped give the structure stability.

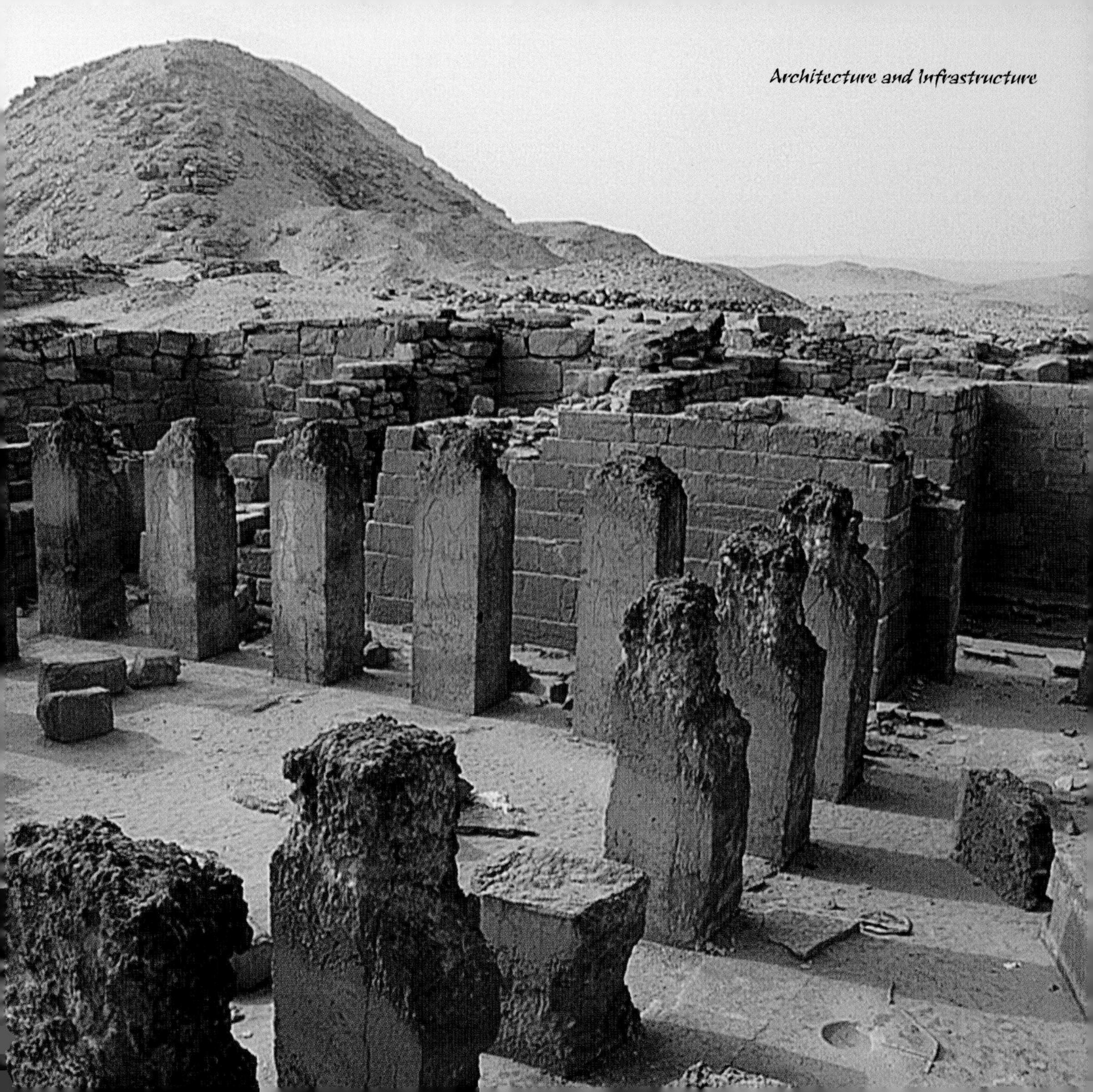

The Tools of Ancient Egyptian Architecture

Viewed from the high-tech standpoint of the 21st century, the tools used by Egyptian architects and craftsmen were primitive in the extreme. Yet they were able to cope with complex architectural methods and, among other great achievements, produce the largest buildings ever constructed.

A simple builder's plumb line allowed Egyptians to delineate vertical lines. Together with an angle, a 52-cm measuring arm and a straight edge, craftsmen could make plans, cross sections and schematic drawings. They could hoist large stone blocks over mud or earth ramps with ropes, levers, rollers and gliders made of wood. The blocks themselves were moulded with nothing stronger than stone pounders or bronze or copper tools. Muscle power also came into play rowing stone-filled boats across the Nile or pulling large boulders to a building site.

Carving and Drilling

Egyptian craftsmen and sculptors used round stone hammers to beat out an overall design. They carved stone with a tool that had a pointed end and used a 'drilling' tool counter-balanced by a bag full of pebbles. Hammered copper sharpened with a sandpaper-type material was used to make cutting devices.

The Fortress of Buhen

During the reign of the 12th-Dynasty king Senusret III (1965–1920 BC), a fortress was built at Buhen in Lower Nubia, near the Second Cataract of the Nile, to protect Egypt's southern border. It stood the furthest north of a series of eight fortresses and included all the latest military technology – a moat dug three metres ($9\frac{4}{5}$ ft) deep into bedrock, together with battlements, ramparts, embrasures, bastions, drawbridges and emplacements for catapults. Inside the fortress, a town was laid out with six major streets arranged on a grid system and rectangular blocks of housing.

Decorating Stone Buildings

The Ancient Egyptians covered the outside walls of their buildings with a mass of hieroglyphs and pictures, all painted in brilliant colours and decorated with ornaments. Many of these ornaments had religious connotations, such as the scarab or sacred beetle which was personified by Khepri, a god of the sun and resurrection. The sun was also in evidence, in the form of a solar disc. So was the vulture, a manifestation of the goddesses Nekhbet and Wadjyt who represented dominion over Upper and Lower Egypt respectively. Palm leaves, the papyrus and the lotus were other motifs commonly used.

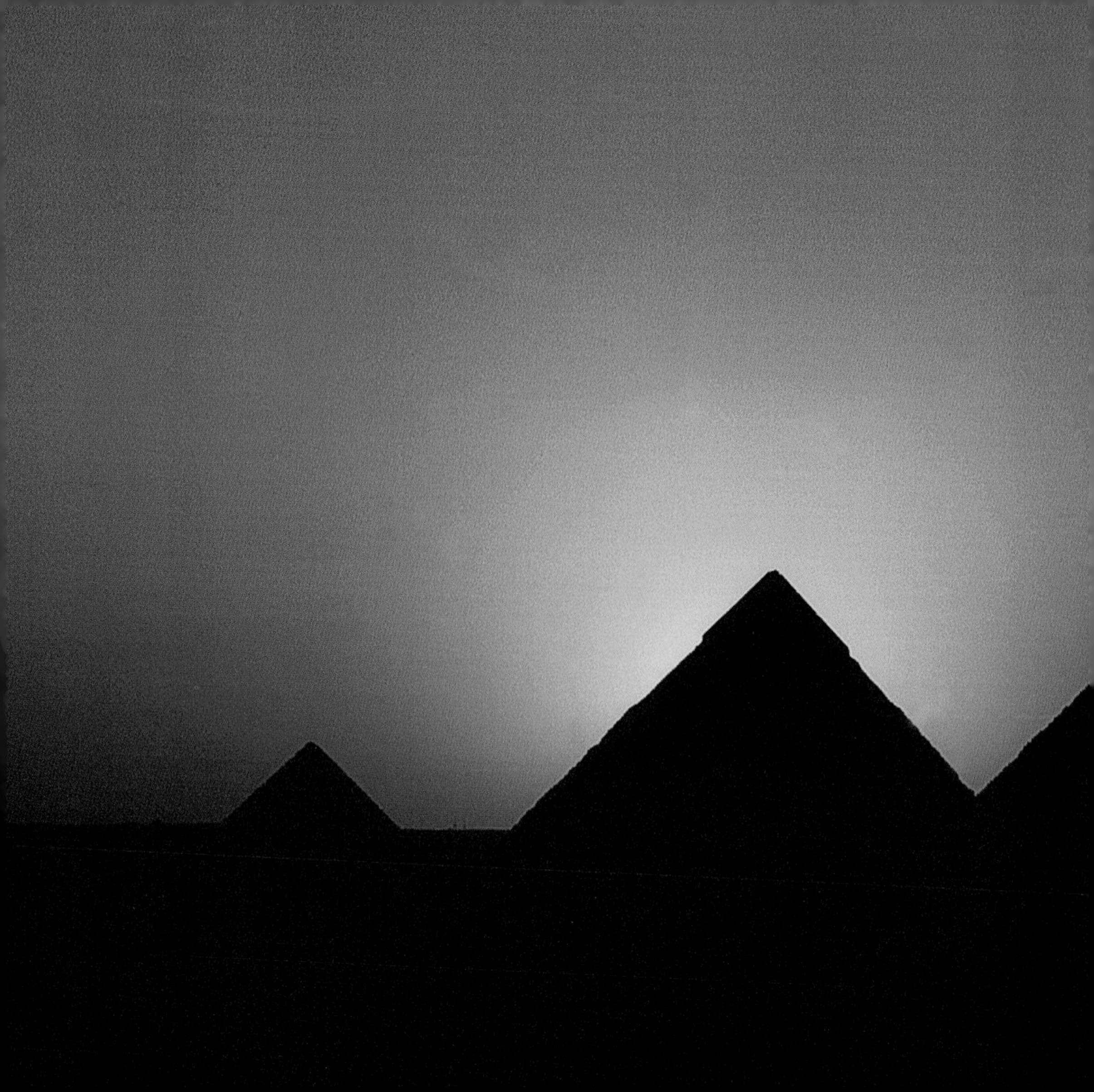

The Pyramids

The pyramids of Ancient Egypt, some of the largest buildings constructed in all history, furnish the most recognizable image of the civilization that flourished beside the River Nile between about 2,500 and 5,000 years ago. Most of the pyramids, which were associated with the royal Sun and Star cults of Egyptian religion, were built during the 1,200 years between the Third Dynasty of the Old Kingdom (2686–2613 BC) and the 16th Dynasty of the Second Intermediate Period (1650–1550 BC). The most prolific construction period was the era of absolute pharaonic rule in the early part of the Fourth Dynasty.

Methods and Materials

The first Ancient Egyptian pyramids had stepped sides, representing stairways to the stars. The steps were later filled in to produce the familiar smooth, sloping appearance. At first, they were constructed of large blocks of limestone, but by the Fifth Dynasty of the Old Kingdom (2494–2345 BC) this had been replaced by small blocks, or loose rubble, faced with finer-cut stone. The expense was now put into the adjacent pyramid temple. Long after the heyday of pyramid building, these monuments were still being constructed, but by the Middle Kingdom (2055–1650 BC), they were made of mud brick covered in polished limestone.

Shape and Symbol

The triangular shape of the pyramids had religious, rather than mathematical or geometric significance. Egyptologists do not agree about the theology behind it. However, it is thought that the pyramid represented the 'primordial mound' which was the first earth to emerge from the waters of chaos at the moment of creation. The triangular side of a pyramid also imitated the rays of the sun shining down on the Earth from a single point in the sky. To emphasise this image, most pyramids were covered in brilliantly reflective white limestone. Also, the Ancient Egyptians believed that a dark region of the night sky which appeared to be the focus of revolving stars was, in fact, a portal to the heavens. In this context, the apex of a pyramid was, as it were, a launch pad that could transport the souls of the dead directly to the home of the gods.

Siting the Pyramids

Most of the pyramids of Ancient Egypt were built in a particular locale that possessed mythical symbolism: on the west bank of the River Nile.

This was the site of the setting Sun, and in Ancient Egyptian mythology, the setting Sun was closely related to the kingdom of the dead.

Who Built the Pyramids?

Contrary to popular belief, the pyramids of Ancient Egypt were not built by slaves lashed to work by cruel taskmasters. Evidence has been uncovered that the pyramid builders included craftsman and specialists, not ordinary labourers, and that they were paid for their services. There was even a special town built to house the workers on the Giza plateau near present-day Cairo. The construction of a pyramid could be a very long-term task – completion might take 20 years or more, which was why pharaohs frequently began the building work soon after they came to the throne. In religious terms, honour and prestige accrued to pyramid builders, but there was also a more prosaic reason behind enlisting for the task. During the annual flooding of the River Nile, there was no farming work to be done so wages earned at the pyramids filled the financial gap for poorer Egyptian families.

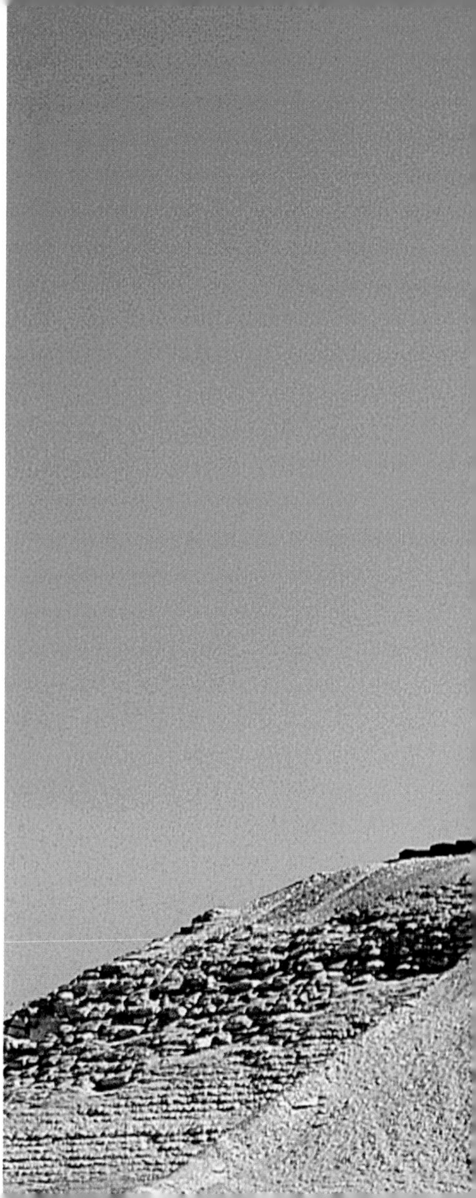

Architecture and Infrastructure

Major Pyramids of Ancient Egypt

Location	Pyramid(s)/Ruler(s)	Era
Abu Rawash	Djedefre	(2566–2558 BC) Fourth Dynasty, Old Kingdom
Giza	*See following pages*	
Zawyet e-Aryan	Nebka	(2686–2667 BC) Third Dynasty, Old Kingdom
	Kaba	(2640–2637 BC) Third Dynasty, Old Kingdom
Abu Sir (three	Sahure	(2487–2475 BC) Fifth Dynasty, Old Kingdom
major pyramids)	Neferirkare Kakai	(2475–2455 BC) Fifth Dynasty, Old Kingdom
	Niuserre	(2455–2421 BC) Fifth Dynasty, Old Kingdom
Saqqara	Djoser	(2667–2648 BC) Third Dynasty, Old Kingdom
	Userkaf	(2494–2487 BC) Fifth Dynasty, Old Kingdom
	Unas	(2375–2345 BC) Fifth Dynasty, Old Kingdom
	Teti	(2345–2323 BC) Sixth Dynasty, Old Kingdom
Dahshur	Sneferu	(2613–2589 BC) Fourth Dynasty, Old Kingdom
	Amenemhat III	(1855–1808 BC) 12th Dynasty, Middle Kingdom
Lisht	Amenemhat I	(1985–1955 BC) 12th Dynasty, Middle Kingdom
	Senusrat I	(1965–1920 BC) 12th Dynasty, Middle Kingdom

The Pyramids of Giza

The three pyramids at Giza which stand on the outskirts of Cairo, the modern Egyptian capital, are the sole survivors of the seven wonders of the ancient world. Constructed during the Fourth Dynasty of the Old Kingdom (2613–2494 BC), they comprise the burial places of three kings: Khufu (2589–2566 BC), his son Khafra (2558–2532 BC) and Khafra's son Menkaure (2532–2503 BC).

The Great Pyramid, originally called 'Khufu is the one belonging to the horizon', is the largest of the three and was constructed from 3.2 million blocks of limestone. Each block weighed on average 2.5 tonnes. Khafra's granite pyramid, once known as 'Great is Khafra', had a subterranean burial chamber, which made it more typical of pyramid design in the Old Kingdom than Khufu's, with its two burial chambers above ground. Menkaure's pyramid, although the smallest, was to have been faced in red granite, but the king died and it was left unfinished.

The Great Sphinx

Together with several small 'queens' pyramids', the Giza complex also includes the Great Sphinx, which is sited next to the causeway of the pyramid where King Khafra (2558–2532 BC) was buried. It acquired its present battered appearance in 1798, when musketeers commanded by the French Emperor Napoleon used it for target practice. It is thought that the Sphinx, which was carved from a rocky mound, represents King Khafra, but the rock was of such poor quality and erosion was such a problem that stone cladding was applied to preserve it. The Sphinx, a term which derived from the expression *shesep ankh* or 'living image', was a mythical beast with the body of a lion and the head of a man: the head of the Great Sphinx was given a nemes headcloth, part of the royal regalia of Ancient Egypt which is also seen on the golden mask of the Pharaoh Tutankhamun (1336–1327 BC).

A Promise in a Dream

Due to its desert location, the Great Sphinx has been buried in sand on many occasions. One of these was commemorated by the 'Dream Stele' set up by Thutmose IV (1400–1390 BC) which recounts how, in a dream, the crown of Egypt was promised to him if he had the sand cleared away.

Thutmose, son of King Amenhotep II, came to the throne as the eighth monarch of the 18th Dynasty in the New Kingdom, (1550–1069 BC). It has been suggested, however, that he was not his father's direct heir, and that therefore Thutmose's 'dream' was a political ploy designed to legitimize his takeover.

Administration in the New Kingdom

By the advent of the New Kingdom in around 1550 BC, the functions assigned to government departments covered three main areas – the dynasty, which comprised the royal family but was actually under the control of the pharaoh, the internal administration and external affairs.

'Family Tree' for Administration in the New Kingdom

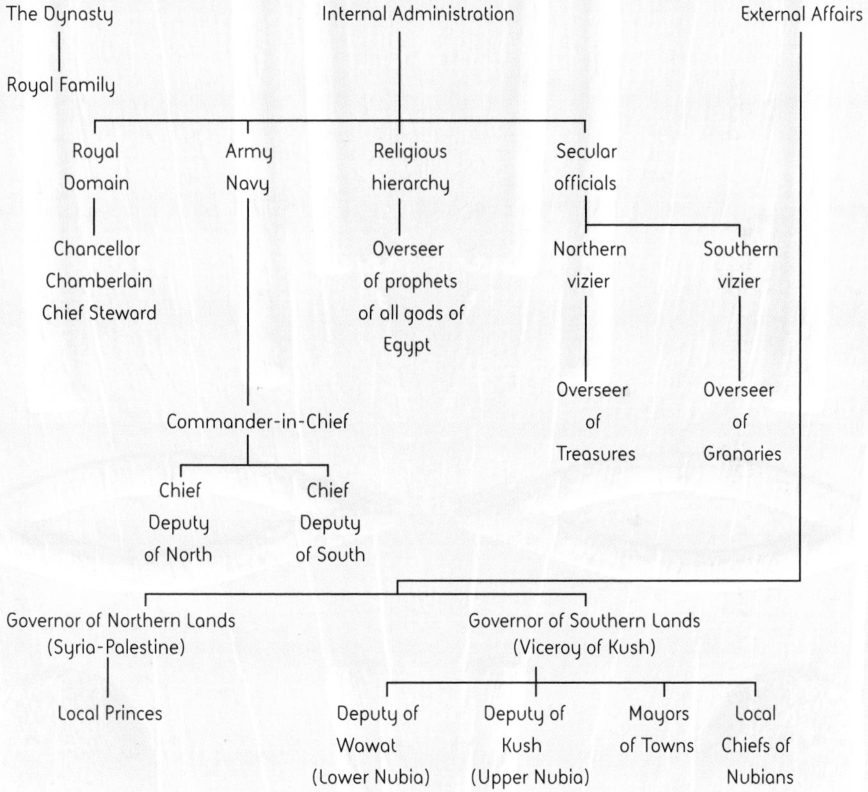
The Dynasty
Royal Family
Internal Administration
External Affairs
Royal Domain
Army Navy
Religious hierarchy
Secular officials
Chancellor Chamberlain Chief Steward
Overseer of prophets of all gods of Egypt
Northern vizier
Southern vizier
Overseer of Treasures
Overseer of Granaries
Commander-in-Chief
Chief Deputy of North
Chief Deputy of South
Governor of Northern Lands (Syria-Palestine)
Local Princes
Governor of Southern Lands (Viceroy of Kush)
Deputy of Wawat (Lower Nubia)
Deputy of Kush (Upper Nubia)
Mayors of Towns
Local Chiefs of Nubians

Bureaucracy in Ancient Egypt

In Ancient Egypt, a large bureaucracy exercised control over most areas of economic activity. The effect of the annual inundation of the River Nile was monitored by 'civil servants' who measured and re-allocated the land after the flooding subsided. They calculated the likely crop yield and collected taxes in kind based on their assessments. Storing grain and other crops and distributing them was another bureaucratic responsibility, as were public works such as the construction of monuments, temples and other religious structures. The bureaucrats organized the huge staff required, comprising sometimes tens of thousands of officials, managers and workmen.

Trade in Ancient Egypt

Once taxes were paid, many households in Ancient Egypt could do as they pleased with surplus produce that remained. Some stored produce for future use and sale. This also applied to any small manufactured goods – jewellery, figurines, toys – which they had made. Such goods were exchanged by barter with other villagers, but there is no evidence for large 'markets' in the modern sense. There were no coins in Egypt until the Late Period (747–332 BC) when they were introduced by Greeks and other foreigners who were already using currency. Local trading was usually small scale, but was a useful element in the Egyptian economy, providing individuals and families with items that might not otherwise be available to them. All foreign trade in luxury goods was in the control of the palace and the temples (that is, the state), which owned ships and sent expeditions to acquire gold, incense and timber in far-off lands.

Working the Land

The great majority of the Egyptian population worked in agriculture. The principle crop was grain, either barley or three kinds of wheat – emmer, einkorn and spelt. Two crops could be grown every year, the first irrigated by the River Nile floods, the second by hand. These second crops usually comprised pulses rather than cereals. Beyond these staples, the Egyptians extracted oils from castor, sesame or flax and also used flax for making textiles. Wine, generally a drink confined to wealthier Egyptians, was made from grapes that grew in profusion in the Nile delta and also in oases in the surrounding desert.

Copper and Bronze

The Egyptians extracted copper ores in the Eastern Desert in Nubia and in the Sinai peninsula. In the Old Kingdom (2686–2181 BC) and Middle Kingdom (2055–1650 BC) copper was smelted by means of reed blow-pipes and crucibles. One of the most spectacular of copper statues, showing a life size Pharaoh Pepi I (2381–2287 BC) was made during the Old Kingdom. Bronze alloy, which combined copper and tin, did not arrive in Egypt until the Middle Kingdom. Technology continued to progress, and in the New Kingdom (1550–1069 BC), leather-covered bellows were being used to facilitate the smelting of both copper and bronze.

Gold

Like copper, gold was mined in the Eastern Desert and Nubia, but the work was so taxing that mining and quarrying were done by criminals guarded by the military. To the Egyptians, gold was more than just another precious metal: they regarded it as the flesh of the Sun-god Ra, whose image was frequently cast in gold. Temples, pyramids, obelisks, funeral masks and coffins were made from or adorned with gold. Gold collars were given by pharaohs to their favourite courtiers during the New Kingdom (1550–1069 BC) and a gold honour, known as the Fly of Valour was awarded to military personnel for bravery in battle.

Silver

The Ancient Egyptians called silver *hedj*, meaning 'white (metal)', or 'bright'. As an import from the Middle East and Mediterranean, it was scarce and even the royal family was forced to 'economize'. For example, Queen Hetepheres (*fl. c.* 2600 BC), the principal wife of Pharaoh Sneferu (2613–2589 BC) wore extremely thin silver bracelets, whereas he was lavishly decorated in a mass of gold jewellery. Silver became more plentiful during the Middle Kingdom (2055–1650 BC) when its value was half that of gold. Like gold, silver had religious connotations for the Ancient Egyptians: they believed it formed the bones of the gods.

Timber and Wood

Wood was a scarce commodity in Ancient Egypt, even though several different species of tree grew there, such as acacia, tamarisk, date palm, sycomore-fig, dom palm and fig. Although they could be used in house and boat building, these trees were mostly unsuitable for high-quality timber, which was imported from Lebanon from the earliest times. Perhaps due to their comparative rarity, some trees became associated with gods and goddesses and the afterlife. The goddess Hathor, for instance, was known as the Lady of the Sycomore-fig.

Tree	Wood used for
Acacia	Boat-building
Ash (imported)	Weapons (e.g. bows)
Cedar (imported from Lebanon)	Sailing ships, higher-class coffins
Date palm	Columns, roof joists, planks
Dom palm	Planks
Ebony (imported from Africa)	Furniture, veneer
Juniper	Architecture, veneer
Sycomore	Coffins, statues
Tamarisk	Coffins, statues

Hierarchy and Eyeliner: Life and Society

Herodotus in Ancient Egypt

Herodotus (*c.* 485–425 BC) was a Greek writer, born in Halicarnassus, whose *Histories* – the result of extensive travels in Asia Minor and the Middle East – contained the first narrative account ever written about events of the past. The book includes a meticulous eyewitness account of the life, people, work, customs and environment of Ancient Egypt, right down to their method of dealing with biting gnats and the thickness of their skulls. According to Herodotus, thick skulls were the result of shaving the head in childhood and exposing it to the sun, which gradually hardened it. Together with the pictorial evidence found by archaeologists in the tombs of Ancient Egypt, the *Histories* provide the first example of 'words and pictures' in world literature.

Herodotus' method, unique in its time, involved thorough research and the verification of facts – he is known as the 'Father of History'.

The Hierarchy of Ancient Egyptian Society According to Herodotus

In Book II of his *Histories*, Herodotus described the 'seven distinct classes' into which Egyptian society was divided:

'There are the priests, the warriors, the cowherds, the swineherds, the tradesmen, the interpreters and the boatmen.' Herodotus noted that the warriors 'had certain privileges in which none of the rest of the Egyptians participated, except the priests. In the first place, each warrior had 12 *arurae* (about four hectares / ten acres) of land assigned to him free of tax.' The warriors, Herodotus wrote 'number, when most numerous, 160 thousand. None of them ever practises a trade, but all are given wholly to war.' Among a range of other privileges which rotated in warrior society – 'the same man never obtaining them twice' – were duty as the bodyguard of the king, and a daily portion of meat and drink consisting of 2.25 kg (5 lb) of baked bread, 1 kg (2 lb 4 oz) of beef and four cups of wine.

Homes in Ancient Egypt

Sun-dried mud bricks were employed to construct ordinary homes two or three storeys high. Floors were commonly made of dried mud. The ground floor was often used as a workshop or business area, with the second and third as living space for the family. The flat roof provided a relatively cool sleeping area in very hot weather. A wealthy or noble family home was more elaborate, with a reception area, a hall and private family quarters. Mats covered doors and windows to keep out flies, the inside walls might be decorated with leather hangings, and the floors were plastered. There was not much furniture in Egyptian homes, just a few stools, chests where clothing, jars, lamps and other paraphernalia were stored and small boxes for keeping jewels and cosmetics.

Status in Seating

Chairs and seating arrangements said a great deal about status, subtly underlining superiority or inferiority. The man who headed a family customarily occupied a higher chair than his wife and children, and the higher ranked official was seated above the lower. Lesser individuals commonly sat on stools, some of them so low to the floor that they were more or less crouching, with their knees up to their chins. The highest chair of all was, of course, occupied by the pharaoh himself. Scenes of banquets show single young men, seated on stools, segregated from the young women, who are given chairs, while the married couples sit together.

How to Frustrate a Gnat, Ancient Egyptian Style

Gnats infested the greater part of Egypt and when the Greek historian and author Herodotus visited the country, he saw how ingenious the inhabitants were in eluding these nasty biting insects.

'The contrivances which they use against gnats, wherewith the country swarms, are the following,' wrote Herodotus. 'In the parts of Egypt above the marshes, the inhabitants pass the night upon lofty towers ... as the gnats are unable to fly to any height on account of the winds. In the marsh country, where there are no towers, each man possesses a net instead. By day, it serves him to catch fish, while at night, he spreads it over (his) bed ... and, creeping in, goes to sleep underneath. The gnats which, if he rolls himself up in his dress or in a piece of muslin, are sure to bite through..., do not so much as attempt to pass the net.'

Family Roles and Women's Work

Family life in Ancient Egypt generally followed a pattern that became the traditional norm for thousands of years afterwards. The Ancient Egyptian husband went out to work, the wife remained at home and looked after the children, the sons were trained to follow their father's trade or craft, and the daughters learned to be housewives. The roles of wife and mother were greatly honoured in Ancient Egypt, for considerable value was placed on the family as the building-block of society.

Nevertheless, there were certain trades and professions open to women. They could run farms and businesses, stepping in where necessary when their husbands or fathers were absent. They manufactured perfumes and were also employed in some of the more glamorous jobs, as acrobats, dancers, singers or musicians at the royal court or in the temples. One job performed by women, which seems strange to us today, was that of professional mourner at funerals.

Family Inheritance in Ancient Egypt

Children were expected to care for elderly parents. In return, after the parents' deaths, offspring enjoyed ample inheritance rights. Sons received the family land, and daughters claimed the household goods, such as furniture or jewellery. If a family had no sons, then the daughters received the land, or even the entire family home.

The Status of Women in Ancient Egypt

The emancipated woman was not exactly common in the ancient world, where the primacy of men was the norm in everyday life and the running of the state. The Ancient Egyptians, however, had a surprisingly liberal attitude in this respect, for even though women were expected to obey their fathers and husbands, they had numerous legal rights. They could take part in business deals. They owned land. They could represent themselves in court cases. They had equal rights in divorce and although their marriages were customarily arranged, their consent had to be obtained before the union could take place.

Beer and Bread

The favourite beverage in Ancient Egypt seems to have been beer, which was usually made from barley. It was once thought that barley bread was fermented to make the beer, but recent investigations suggest that the barley was allowed to shoot, and that was brewed with natural yeasts. A range of flavourings could be added, including dates.

Bread to eat was a much finer product than this. Emmer-wheat was ground into flour and pounded to turn it into fine grain. Before baking, the dough was flavoured with honey, fruit, herbs, butter or sesame seeds.

Food and Cooking in Ancient Egypt

The Egyptians used wood-fired clay ovens to cook food, or cooked over open fires, usually in a courtyard as they did not like the cooking smells in the house. Serving dishes made of silver, gold or bronze were reserved for the rich, while everyone else used clay. The utensils for preparing and cooking food found in Egyptian excavations include pots, pans, ladles, whisks, sieves and storage jars.

Poorer Egyptians lived mainly on vegetables – onions, garlic, lettuce, beans, cucumbers – and fish. They also ate what they could hunt, such as hares or gazelles, while domestic pigs provided meat for the poor class of Egyptian. Livestock were kept for their milk, which was used to make cheese and ducks and geese provided a supply of eggs. Fruits were plentiful, such as dates, figs, grapes, dôm-palm nuts and pomegranates. Bee-keeping furnished the Egyptians with honey, the staple sweetener of ancient times.

Cleanliness in Ancient Egypt

The Egyptians were greatly concerned with keeping clean and smelling sweet. Most went to the River Nile for a daily bath or washed from basins of water at home. In a wealthy household, servants would pour jugs of water over their master as he sat in a 'bath', which had a pipe that enabled the water to drain away. Cleansing cream was made from an astringent mixture of oil, perfume and lime, and the skin was also rubbed with perfumed oil made from flowers and scented woods. The oils prevented the skin from drying out in the often fiercely hot climate.

Making-up in Ancient Egypt

As paintings on the pyramid tomb walls reveal, both men and women wore make-up. Worn on the eyelids in the form of green malachite-based paint or black kohl with a line extending to the hairline on either side, make-up had medical, religious and even magical connotations. Many Egyptians believed that eye make-up had healing powers to fight eye infections, improve bad eyesight and reduce damage done by the glare of the sun. Red ochre was ground and mixed with water to redden cheeks and lips, and yellow-orange henna was used as nail varnish. An all-important adjunct to make up was a mirror, and many examples, in highly polished silver or copper, have been found in tombs. Make-up was so important in Egypt that people were buried with their cosmetics. Women, it seems, took their make up boxes with them to parties.

Wearing Wigs

Most Egyptians kept their own hair short, but also wore wigs made of sheep's wool or human hair. Some wigs were for decoration or were added to real hair to make it more attractive. Some were meant to protect both head and hair from the intense heat of the sun.

Clothes and Jewellery

Clothing in Ancient Egypt was generally simple, even basic, whereas jewellery was very elaborate. Most clothing was made of linen. Men wore short skirts, or 'kilts', women wore straight tunic dresses with straps over the shoulders. More elaborate fashions came in with the New Kingdom (1550–1069 BC) when nobles wore long robes and women, long pleated dresses and shawls. For most people, sandals were for special occasions. Most of the time, men and women went barefoot and in the summer, children ran about naked. Dressing – or not dressing – was a sensible way of countering the hot, dry climate. Jewellery, such as rings or amulets, was believed to provide protection against injury or evil spirits. Other jewellery included armlets, bracelets, anklets, earrings, necklaces, pendants and, for the rich, pieces inlaid with gold, silver, turquoise, lapis lazuli or carnelian. Poorer Egyptians wore jewellery made of copper or faience, a ceramic made from crushed quartz.

Marriage in Ancient Egypt

There appears to have been no temple-based wedding ceremony in Ancient Egypt, and the marriage was marked by the bride joining her husband in his house. Elite marriage contracts do survive, and brides took a dowry with them (which was returned if they divorced). Because of the brevity of life in ancient times, both husband and wife married very young, the girl probably at around 14 years of age, the husband between around 17 and 20.

The arranged marriage was common, with the bride's father having the major say in the arrangement. But love matches were also frequent, as evidenced by the mass of love poetry in Egyptian literature. Many paintings and sculptures show couples holding hands, embracing or exchanging romantic gifts, such as flowers or food. In statues and tomb paintings, wives are shown as eternally youthful, slim and beautiful, and wearing their finest clothes.

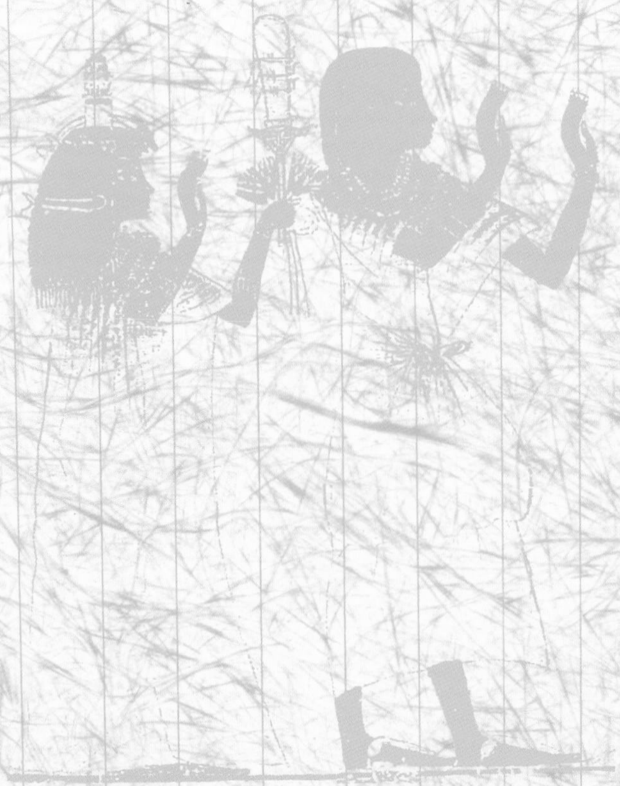

Marriage Contracts

One marriage contract found among the records left by the Ancient Egyptians listed six items of information required from the parties concerned. First came the date, which comprised the reign year of the current king or pharaoh, then the names of the couple and those of their parents. The husband's profession was listed, along with the name of the scribe who drew up the contract and the names of the witnesses. A couple would not receive their own copy of the marriage contract, however. This was given to a third party for safekeeping or else was lodged among the records of the local temple.

Divorce in Ancient Egypt

Divorce was permitted in Egyptian society and could be initiated by either partner. Husbands divorced wives who had failed to produce children or most importantly a son, or simply if he tired of her and wanted someone else. Wives opted for divorce on grounds of mental or physical cruelty or because their husbands had committed adultery. Before the final step was taken, though, a couple's families were enlisted to attempt a reconciliation. Divorce followed if these efforts failed.

There was no ceremony. Divorce consisted of a simple statement made in front of witnesses that the 'marriage' was over. Usually, the wife was given custody of the children. Her former husband was obliged to support her and the children, often handing over about one third of his income.

Childbirth in Ancient Egypt

Childbirth was a dangerous process in Ancient Egypt and the safety of both mother and child was uncertain. A range of prayers and spells was used to produce a favourable outcome. Good-luck charms, magic amulets and small images of the gods served to preserve a newborn and fend off evil influences. The Egyptian language had no word for specialists in childbirth – midwife or gynaecologist – but archaeological evidence indicates the existence of these professions, and the 'Kahun Papyrus' (*c.* 1800 BC) contains guidance relevant to their task. This document contains 17 prescriptions for drugs of assistance in childbirth and instructions on how to facilitate the birth itself. In case the infant failed to survive more than a few minutes or hours after birth, mothers would name them as soon as they were born. In Ancient Egypt, without a name, an infant was non-existent and would be denied a future in the afterlife.

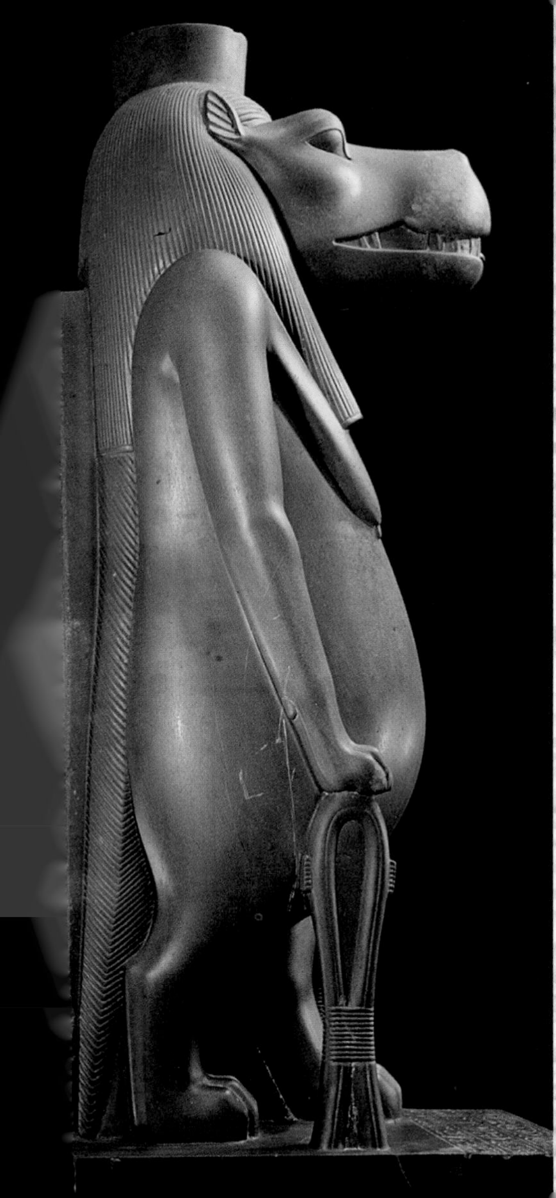

Children in Ancient Egypt

Despite the many benefits of its Nile location, environment and fertility, survival in Ancient Egypt was a matter of chance. Egyptologists have excavated enough child graves to prove the fragility of life, even in this most favoured of places and the Egyptian family, averaging perhaps nine children, could expect to lose three or four of them before they reached maturity. Infant mortality was particularly high and there were specific magic spells designed to sustain a newborn's only source of survival, their mothers' milk. In Ancient Egyptian art, children were often depicted naked, with a finger in their mouths and during and after the Old Kingdom (2686–2181 BC) the pre-pubescent among them, both boys and girls, wore a 'Sidelock of Youth' until they were around 10 years old. A child's head was customarily shaved, except for a single long tress that was plaited and hung over one ear.

Education in Ancient Egypt

The majority of Ancient Egyptians were unable to read or write. Writing, and the access to knowledge that came with it, was carefully cherished as a preserve of the ruling elite. All of Egypt's officials were first of all 'scribes', keeping records and accounts in triplicate – or even quadruplicate. The entire system depended on being able to keep surplus food and distribute it in times of shortage.

Schools, where they existed, were designed for boys; and what we call the Three R's were learnt by rote, copying out examples, and committing long texts to memory. Boys first learned the hieratic script used for religious texts, but afterwards adapted for use in business transactions. Discipline in schools was very strict, so much so that it gave rise to the saying: 'A boy's ear is on his back – he listens when he is beaten.'

153

Playing Games

'Draughts' in Ancient Egypt

The most popular board game in Ancient Egypt was senet, a forerunner of the modern game of draughts or checkers. The aim of the game, which was played on a chequered board containing three rows of 10 squares each, was to get individual pieces round a track that snaked through the board. On the way, players might encounter 'good' or 'bad' fortune squares. Senet was a game for two players, each with seven pieces of different shapes or colours. Astragals (knuckle bones) or casting sticks were thrown to decide how many squares a piece covered in the race to finish first.

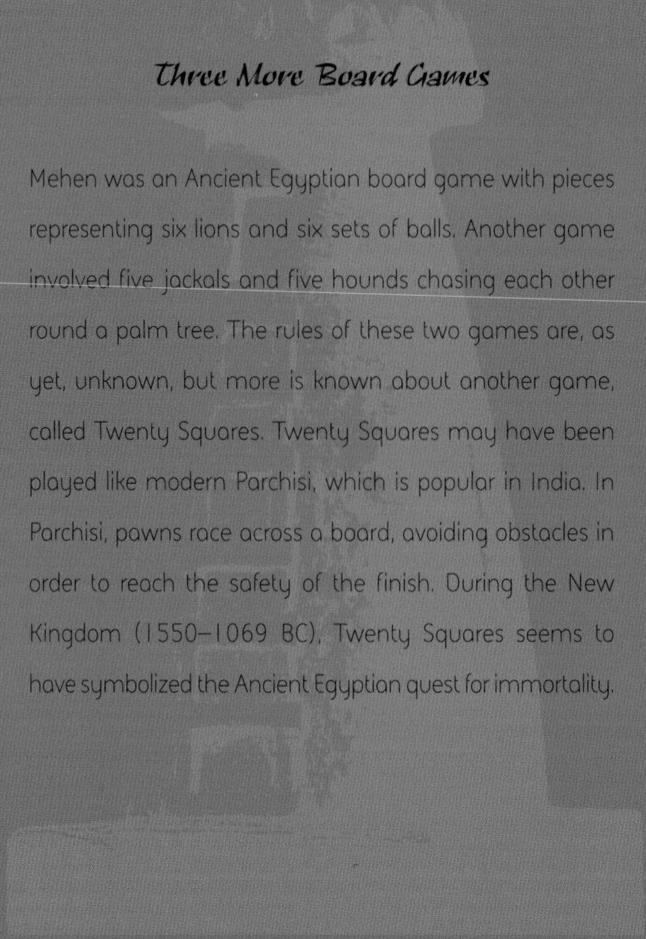

Three More Board Games

Mehen was an Ancient Egyptian board game with pieces representing six lions and six sets of balls. Another game involved five jackals and five hounds chasing each other round a palm tree. The rules of these two games are, as yet, unknown, but more is known about another game, called Twenty Squares. Twenty Squares may have been played like modern Parchisi, which is popular in India. In Parchisi, pawns race across a board, avoiding obstacles in order to reach the safety of the finish. During the New Kingdom (1550–1069 BC), Twenty Squares seems to have symbolized the Ancient Egyptian quest for immortality.

Board Games in Religion

Games have featured in several civilizations – Ancient Rome, prehispanic Mexico – as an adjunct to religious rituals, and board games may have served this function in Ancient Egypt. It is thought that games for two players may have been intended to reflect the journey made by the dead through the underworld.

Ancient Egyptian Toys

For many families, Ancient Egypt was an affluent society and children had plenty of toys to play with. Ball games were played with balls made of moulded papyrus. Children had dolls modelled on people or animals, wooden spinning tops and rattles. Toys even had moving parts – such as crocodiles with movable jaws. A problem with many figures of people and animals excavated in Egyptian tombs is that these objects could have had religious rather than recreational significance, for small figurines or statuettes were habitually used in the practices of the many religious cults in Ancient Egypt. They were important, too, in Egyptian magic.

21805

Competitive Sport in Ancient Egypt

The Egyptians enjoyed several energetic sports, like boxing, wrestling or fencing with sticks. Long before the more familiar Olympic Games of Ancient Greece were held, the Egyptians had their own competition featuring similar sports – hockey, gymnastics, weightlifting, archery, rowing, long-distance running, high jump, tug of war, handball and spear-throwing. The River Nile was the centre of many sporting activities – fishing, swimming or boat games in which two teams pushed each other with long poles to upend their rivals into the water. The Egyptians also hunted hippopotamuses and crocodiles and, less perilously, enjoyed leisurely days out simply boating on the river.

A Show of Strength

Some Egyptian pharaohs greatly prided themselves on their sporting prowess. A stela near the Great Sphinx at Giza describes the skill of Amenhotep II (1427–1400 BC), seventh king of the 18th Dynasty, in archery, athletics, rowing and horseriding. A mural in the step pyramid tomb at Saqqara belonging to Djoser, a ruler (2667–2648 BC) of the Third Dynasty, shows him running between two sets of three cairns at the Sed festival of regeneration. The cairns may have represented the boundaries of Djoser's realm, but the figure of Djoser himself was clearly that of a trained athlete, with rippling muscles and an interplay of arms, legs and trunk that suggests a regular fitness regime. These examples of physical prowess at the top of Egyptian society had a considerable effect on the rest of society. The figure in general portrayed in painting and sculpture was an ideal: people were fine physical specimens – the men vigorous and muscular, the women slender and feminine.

Amenhotep II – The Sporting King

King Amenhotep II (*c.* 1427–1400 BC), who reigned during the 18th Dynasty of the New Kingdom (1550–1069 BC) was one of the first monarchs of Ancient Egypt to enjoy early acquaintance with the sporting world. The image of royal sportsman-athlete and dashing prince was one that he relished and he gave much publicity to this aspect of his role as ruler. Amenhotep's particular sporting interest was horses. When he was still a boy, his father King Thutmose III (1470–1425 BC) put him in charge of the royal stables. Before long, Amenhotep was an expert horseman and archer and became skilled as a mounted bowman, which brought him great success in hunting. King Amenhotep demonstrated equal prowess as an oarsman, and regularly competed in the sport with one of his army officers, Ahmose. Amenhotep was, needless to say, a formidable warrior-monarch who put his sporting prowess to effective use when triumphing over the enemies of Egypt.

Ancient Egyptian Music

Music was of considerable importance in the life of Ancient Egypt from early on. Pictorial evidence was found on numerous vessels and palettes used in religious ceremonies dating from the Predynastic era. Later, during the New Kingdom (1550–1069 BC), musical instruments ranged from simple clappers made of ivory to tambourines, harps and lutes played by girls at banquets or open-air celebrations. Cymbals, bells and sistra (rattling instruments) were frequently played at religious services. Drums were sometimes used in religious processions, although their principle use, like bugles and trumpets, was for military music. Musicians also played some instruments similar to simple versions of the flute, clarinet and oboe.

An Egyptian orchestra or ensemble included string instruments with open strings, like the lyre and harp, and those with 'stopped' strings, such as the guitar or lute, wind instruments, including the flute, pipe and trumpet, and percussion instruments such as drums, clappers and bells.

Ancient Egyptian Dance

Music and dance went together in Ancient Egyptian life, and pairs of female dancers were a frequent subject for Egyptian artists. Scenes of musicians accompanying dancers appear in tomb paintings, and the dancers followed the rhythm with hand-held castanets. Their moves incorporated acrobatics such as cartwheels, hand-stands and other athletic movements. Dance had great ritual significance, as revealed by the muu-dancers in skirts and reed crowns, who performed alongside funeral processions. Artists sometimes provided dancing 'lessons' in their paintings and murals, by depicting a line of figures, representing a single performer moving through a series of dance steps.

Singing in Honour of the Gods

As well as being a popular entertainment at banquets and public celebrations, singing was regarded as a way of honouring the gods. Religious services, ceremonies and processions were accompanied by singing, and one god, Amun, had a special singer known as 'Chantress to Amun'. This was a much-sought-after role for women who had to belong to the elite class to qualify.

Poems and songs are preserved in a range of ancient sources. Some were written on tomb walls, accompanying a picture of a harpist, showing that they were sung. Love poems are written from the perspective of both man and woman, and show all the usual anguish and anticipation. Examples of love songs have been found in the village of Deir el-Medina, dating from the Ramesside era of the New Kingdom (*c.* 1550–1069 BC).

Art: An Obsession with Life

The Concept of Art in Ancient Egypt

A culture as dominated by religion as Ancient Egypt during the time of the pharaohs had little room for the concept of 'art for art's sake' or for purely representational painting or sculpture. It has sometimes been said that the Egyptians were obsessed with death, but it would be far truer to say that they were obsessed with life. This is why they put so much time, wealth, energy and expertise into using art for the purpose of perpetuating life and even of replacing it. A certain element of fantasy was involved, not only in the idealized figures of pharaohs and other dignitaries found inside pyramid tombs, but in the depiction of meat, fish, fruit and other foods: this was supposed to transform into the real thing once the food left in the tomb ran out.

Style in Ancient Egyptian Art

The instructions given to Ancient Egyptian artists were designed to achieve a style of art that was complete and exact – any attractiveness or structures pleasing to the eye were happy bi-products of this. The Egyptians feared chaos and their overriding aim was art that reflected order and balance. To achieve this impression, simple lines and simple shapes were used. Grids comprising vertical and horizontal lines were employed to ensure that images were given their correct proportions. The size of an image was also vital in conveying the relative importance of the person concerned. A pharaoh, for instance, was depicted much larger than anyone else in a picture, with no regard paid to more modern concerns like proportion or perspective. The pharaoh's wife was shown noticeably smaller and her children smaller still. Equally, an important god, such as Amun, was represented larger than a lesser member of the Ancient Egyptian pantheon.

180

Painting People in Ancient Egypt

Egyptian artists were not much concerned with the realistic representation of figures. The human image was designed from a series of separate elements, each representing the most complete, ideal and recognizable views. So the face was shown in profile, to give a clear image, with a complete nose, but with the eye viewed full on. Both shoulders were shown, but with a profile of the chest, back, legs and feet. In addition, faces had little or no individuality. The effect was highly stylized, but as far as the artist was concerned, it was done according to longstanding tradition.

Warts and All

For almost all the many centuries in which kings and pharaohs were depicted by Ancient Egyptian artists, they were given idealized images, with perfect forms and neat, symmetrical features. Making pharaohs or their queens look good was the most important instruction issued to artists and it was followed to the letter. There were, however, a few years during the 'Amarna period' (1352–1336 BC) when Akhenaten was pharaoh and artists were allowed to paint him as they saw him. Unfortunately therefore, Akhenaten appeared complete with pot belly, long head and long face. But the art of the Amarna period also provided a new, more human view of Akhenaten's family. They were depicted as people who were fond of each other rather than in the stylized, formal severity of the traditional royal portrait. Once Akhenaten died, the pharaoh in art reverted to this tradition and naturalism in Ancient Egyptian portraiture was over.

Sculpture as a Statement of Power

A statue of King Khafra who reigned during the Fourth Dynasty of the Old Kingdom (*c.* 2558–2532 BC) and built the second pyramid at Giza, appears to be a straightforward carving of a very powerful and impressive monarch seated in majesty on an elaborate throne. It is deceptively simple however, as the statue, which is made of diorite, a speckled, coarse-grained igneous rock, features symbols that say a great deal more about Khafra and his illustrious place in the early history of Ancient Egypt. Hawk's wings behind his head and neck represent Horus, Khafra's divine alter ego as ruler. Khafra ruled over Upper and Lower Egypt, and the extent of his power is symbolized by decorations on either side of his throne which feature a hieroglyph meaning 'union', bound up in the tendrils of plants representing the two regions of his kingdom.

Rules for Sculptors

The strict traditions involved in Ancient Egyptian sculpture ensured that even after 3,000 years and more, the appearance of statues changed hardly at all. According to the rules, a statue of a man was darker than a statue of a woman. If the subject was sitting down, he or she had to be shown with hands on knees. The Egyptian gods had their own individual conventions. Horus, the sky god, had to be represented with the head of a falcon. Anubis, god of funerals and their rites, was always given the head of a jackal. However, these conventions in art and statuary did not reflect a lack of imagination on the part of Egyptian sculptors. The rules existed to impart a certain timelessness and a lack of ageing in the *ka*, the life spirit, of the subject so that the sculpture's subject could enter the afterlife in fresh and youthful condition.

Art

Ancestor Busts

Ancestors were revered throughout Egyptian history. During the New Kingdom (1550–1069 BC) small busts of ancestors served as a focus for this reverence. They were mostly made of limestone or sandstone although wood and clay were also used. Around 150 busts have been excavated by archaeologists, about half of them at the village of Deir el-Medina, on the west bank of the Nile opposite Luxor. Dead ancestors were designated *akh iker en Ra*, 'excellent spirit of Ra', and also appeared on some 55 painted stelae. Relatives seeking aid from the gods would address their requests to the busts and stelae.

Block Statues in Ancient Egypt

In Ancient Egypt, during the Middle Kingdom (2055–1650 BC), individuals were depicted in a squatting position with their knees underneath their chins. The effect was to render the body into a square shape, although in some statues, the sculptor managed to indicate the outlines of the individual's legs. The purpose of a block statue was to present the individual as a sentinel, guarding the entrance to a temple. During the Late Period (747–323 BC) block statues became a popular cult because they provided an ample surface on which to identify the individual and give prayers for his continued existence.

The Dyad – Togetherness in Sculpture

The 'togetherness' of the Ancient Egyptian dyad, a double- or pair-statue had several interpretations. These statues, usually carved from a single block of stone or other material, might depict a husband and wife, sometimes with their children around their legs. Alternatively the two images could be two versions of an individual. Another purpose was to represent the physical and the spiritual aspects of a single subject. A granite dyad of Amenemhat III (1855–1808 BC) excavated at Tanis in the Nile Delta between 1883 and 1886 is thought by some Egyptologists to represent the human and divine aspects of the Pharaoh.

The Statue of Ka-Aper

Although so much of Ancient Egyptian art was stylized, and faces seemed to have little individuality, there were some works of art that were more lifelike. Among them was the life-sized statue of Ka-Aper (also known as Sheikh el-Beled), a chief lector-priest, which was uncovered in Saqqara, near Memphis, by the French archaeologist Auguste Mariette (1821–81). Carved from sycomore-fig wood, with eyes made of rock-crystal and copper, the statue depicts a burly, thick-set man about 50 years of age, wearing a straight skirt and holding a staff in his left hand and a sekhem sceptre in his right. The likely date of the statue has been disputed, but most scholars believed that Ka-Aper lived around 2500 BC, during the Fourth Dynasty of the Old Kingdom.

What's in a Name?

The Ancient Egyptian word for a sculptor meant 'he who keeps alive', emphasizing the symbolic significance of his tangible art.

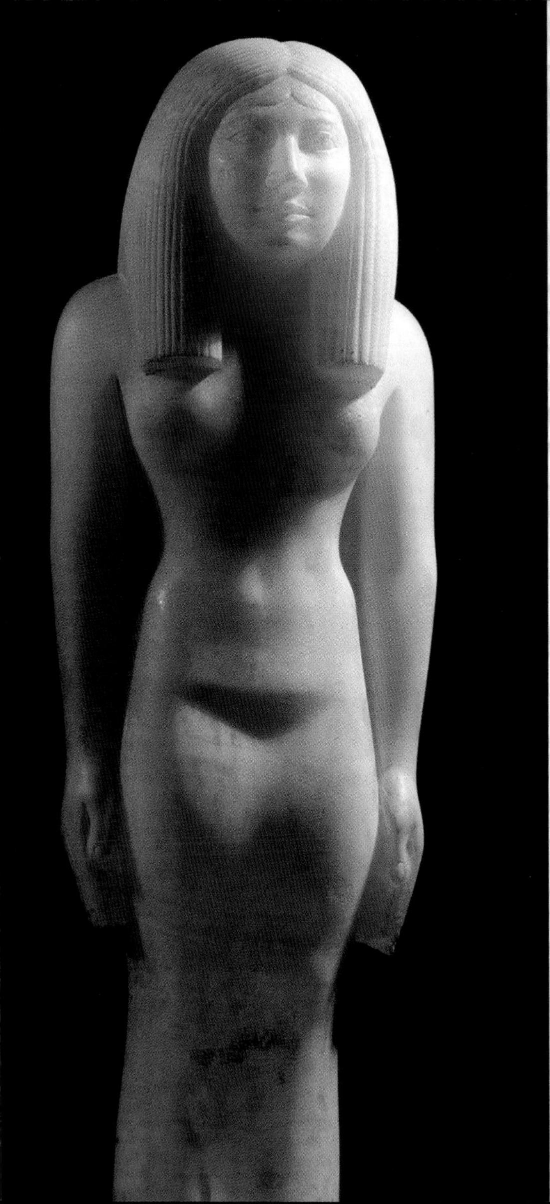

Artists in Ancient Egypt

Although the Egyptian language had a word for 'sculptor', there was none for 'artist'. Even though artists appeared in some of the tomb scenes they themselves created, the lack of their own title underlined the fact that they were anonymous. Their work, however beautifully done, however greatly appreciated, was more important than they were. While individual artists and sculptors remained unnamed, it was imperative for each painting or sculpture to be identified as an image of the person it depicted, so that it could serve its religious function in perpetuating his or her life after death. All work was commissioned by the king or the elite, and artists generally worked in teams under the eagle eye of an overseer who ensured that they followed strict guidelines in whatever work they produced. Sons were often apprenticed to their fathers and in time inherited their jobs.

The Opening of the Mouth

'Opening the mouth' was a religious ritual designed to bring a deceased person to life so that their *ka*, the life force, could return to the body. 'Art' was involved in the form of a statue of the deceased, which, in addition to the mummy, was touched on the face with special implements.

Protective Symbolism in Art

Anything and everything an artist or sculptor might create had a potent life of its own. When completed, the scenes in tombs and temples were 'activated' through religious rites. In the Old Kingdom when dangerous animals appeared as hieroglyphics they had to be neutralized from harming the tomb owner. This could be done by mutilating them – so the dangerous parts were shown as if cut off. Another way was to show, for example, a crocodile or a lion with a knife in its back, symbolically 'killing' the hieroglyph and rendering it harmless.

Ancient Egyptian Art Across the Centuries

Approx. date	Period	Type of art produced
8000 BC	Prehistoric	Engraved drawings on cliffs of hunting scenes, wild game
5550–3100 BC	Predynastic	Grave goods carved in ivory or stone, small votive human figurines
3100–2686 BC	Late Predynastic	Decorated maces, flint knives with ivory handles, cosmetic and ceremonial palettes
2686–2181 BC	Old Kingdom	Tomb sculpture, painted reliefs, 'power' statues, richly decorated tombs of provincial governors
2055–1650 BC	Middle Kingdom	In tombs, scenes of sports (hunting, fishing, wrestling) or scenes of battle

1650–1550 BC	Hyksos (invaders) (15th Dynasty)	Kept to traditional Egyptian reliefs and sculptures, but imported influences in painting from the Minoan civilization of Crete
1550–1352/ 1336–1069 BC (see below for interval)	New Kingdom	Painted tombs and statuary in the Valley of the Kings, and the temples of Karnak, Luxor, Medinet Habu and Deir el-Bahri
1352–1336 BC	Amarna period	Paintings, statues monopolized by images of Aten, the Sun god championed by Akenaten
1069–332 BC	Intermediate/ Late Period	Efforts to revive art of the Old and Middle Kingdom at a time of political instability, ending in 323 BC with the conquest of Egypt by Alexander the Great

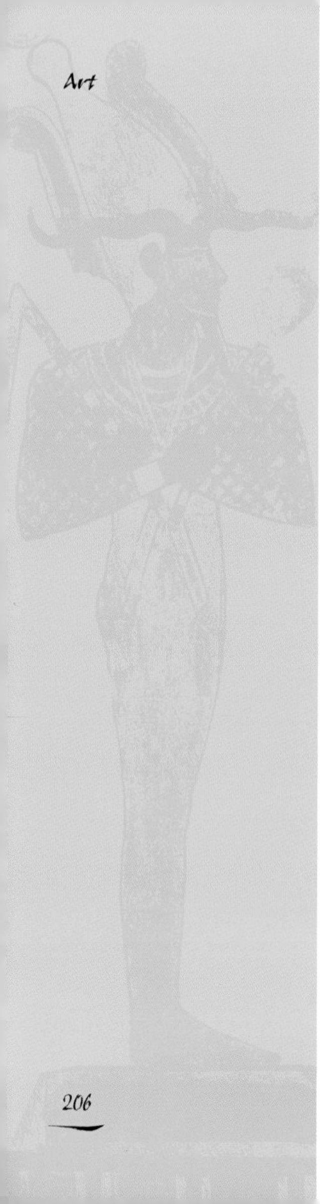

The Symbolism of Colour

In Ancient Egypt, colour denoted the substance of every thing and every person in life and each colour had its own symbolic significance. It followed that the use of colour in art was not just to please the eye, but to symbolize the quality and nature of the subject. Amun, the chief god in the Egyptian pantheon, was shown with a blue skin, reflecting his cosmic importance. In his portraits, Osiris, the god of death, resurrection and fertility was given a green skin because of his connection with vegetation and the annual re-emergence of plant life. Seth, god of chaos and confusion, who murdered Osiris, was painted red to imply anger and the violence of war. White denoted purity and omnipotence, and was the colour used in religious objects, such as ceremonial bowls.

Colours and their Meanings

Colour	Egyptian name	Denoted
Green	Wadj	Vegetation and new Life
Red	Desher	Life and victory
White	Hedj/shesep	Omnipotence and purity
Black	Kem	Death and Night
Yellow (gold)	Khenet/kenit	The eternal, indestructible
Blue	Letiu/sbedj	Creation, heaven, sky, water

How Artists Created Colours in Ancient Egypt

Colour	Made from
Green	Copper and iron oxides, plus silica and calcium or malachite
Red	Oxidized iron and red ochre
White	Chalk and gypsum
Black	Soot, ground charcoal or burned animal bones
Yellow (gold)	Ochres and oxides, or orpiment (arsenic trisulphide)
Blue	Copper and iron oxides, plus silica and calcium

Colourful language

The imagery of colour produced colloquialisms in the Ancient Egyptian language. To act in a 'green fashion' was slang for good or beneficial behaviour. If someone 'acted with a red heart', they were in a rage and 'to redden' did not mean to become embarrassed: instead, it meant 'to die'.

How Pictures were Painted

Preliminary sketches were made on flakes of stone, or on papyrus. The artist often outlined the scene, in red, directly onto the wall with only a few guidelines, although sometimes the wall was covered in a grid. A coarse brush made of palm fibres was employed to paint large areas – or the artist used a brush made of pieces of wood chewed or beaten to soften them. Each colour in a painting had its own brush. Paintings were rendered without perspective and in flat colours, although shading was used sometimes.

The Pharaoh Smites his Enemies

For Egyptian pharaohs, displays of power were a vital part of their image. This is what made scenes of pharaohs smiting their enemies such a constant feature of Egyptian art after *c.* 1550 BC and the advent of the New Kingdom. However, as early as the Predynastic (5500–3100 BC) or Early Dynastic (3100–2686 BC) periods, there were depictions of Egyptian kings personally executing or humiliating bound captives. Pictures of this kind persisted for centuries, well into the time when Egypt was ruled by the Romans (30 BC– AD 395). This type of art played an important part in promoting the concept of the omnipotent Egyptian pharaoh.

Surviving the Millennia

Egypt has proved a particularly suitable place for the preservation of ancient paintings in virtually new condition. A very dry climate has ensured that the fading, darkening or colour changing that can affect works of art in more humid environments has barely affected the art of Ancient Egypt, even after thousands of years.

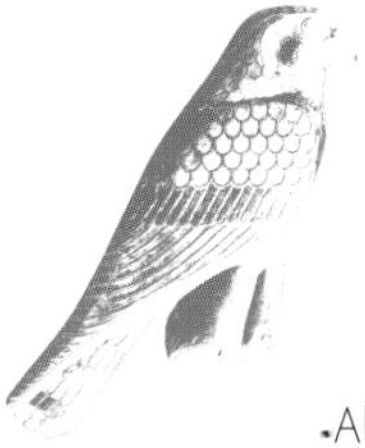

Animals in Ancient Egyptian Religious Art

Although the Egyptians did not worship animals, animals were represented in hunting and decorative scenes but were particularly used in religious art to demonstrate divine characteristics. Horus was pictured with a falcon's head because he was thought to possess the tenacity, courage and keen eye of that particular bird. Some Egyptian deities shared the same image. The goddess Sekhmet, whose name meant 'she who is powerful', was depicted as a lioness, reflecting the courage and ferocity of the animal. Yet, the lioness image also featured in portraits of Bestet, the cat goddess, Mut, the vulture goddess and Hathor, the bovine goddess to reflect the protective, mothering aspects of this animal.

Hieroglyphs and Art

In Ancient Egypt, there was a strong connection between hieroglyphs and what we would regard as visual art, as the meaning of pictures provided the basis for the Egyptian writing system. Among the boys trained as scribes, tutors kept a special eye out for the most gifted of their pupils, those who were capable of producing artistic hieroglyphs for inclusion on pictures or portraits. In some of the pyramid tombs, hieroglyphs were embellished to look more like complete 'pictures'. Of course this might be for more than aesthetic purposes. Examples are those hieroglyphs representing dangerous animals, like snakes, being shown mangled, stabbed or otherwise disabled so that they would not prove a danger to the incumbent.

At the Mercy of the Gods: Religion and Mythology

Worship in Ancient Egypt

Egyptian culture and religion developed in a hostile world (8,000–3,000 BC). The dessication of the Sahara forced people – probably cattle herders – towards the Nile Valley, and a more sedentary, agricultural way of life. But the annual flooding of the river on which agriculture depended was itself unpredictable. The spirits who controlled the natural phenomena needed to be placated to ensure the continuing cycle of seasons and a beneficial flood. Over time the Egyptians 'discovered' more and more gods with specific attributes and functions. They also developed an increasingly personal relationship with certain gods who were thought to help with overcoming illnesses, and death itself. In the Nile Delta, people adopted Horus, god of the sky. Elsewhere, Osiris, god of death and resurrection, was the preferred deity. Eventually, there emerged a pantheon which became so extensive that a 'hierarchy' of deities developed.

The Hierarchy of the Gods

Local deities proliferated, for Egypt comprised a mass of individual regions each with its own traditions, customs – and gods. However, local gods could be 'promoted' to national status if their locality acquired extra importance and their cults spread countrywide. This is what happened, for example, to Ptah, the creator-god who originated in Memphis; Amun of Thebes, described as the 'king of the gods' who came from Karnak; and Ra the Sun god who was first worshipped in Heliopolis.

The eminence of a particular god or goddess also depended on the beliefs of individual kings or pharaohs, and where they established their capital cities. This was how the Pharaoh Amenhotep IV or Akhenaten (1352–1366 BC) managed to give Aten, the Sun Disk, a monopoly of faith in Egypt during his reign and made Karnak and his new city of Akhetaten the focus of his worship instead of the traditional centres, Memphis and Thebes.

The Gods of Ancient Egypt

Fragmented beliefs in Ancient Egypt created a patchwork of gods and goddesses, about 2,000 in all, in which some deities had more than one name and more than one deity represented a single element or factor in life.

Name: Amun/Amun-Ra
Role: King of the Gods
Origin: Hermopolis/Thebes

Name: Anubis
Role: Canine god of embalming and burial
Origin: Kynopolis

Name: Apis

Role: Physical manifestation of Ptah (creator god)

Origin: Memphis

Name: Aton/Aten

Role: Sun god (promoted by Pharaoh Amenhotep IV, 1352–1336 BC)

Origin: Akhetaten/Tell el-Amarna

Name: Atum/Re-Atum

Role: Creator god/Sun god

Origin: Heliopolis

Name: Hathor

Role: Goddess of love, dance, alcohol. Also goddess of the dead, the sky and cows

Origin: Thebes

Name: Horus

Role: Earliest royal god, sky god, ruler of the day. Among alternative names for Horus, one – Khentekhtay – was a crocodile god, another – Harmakhis – was 'Horus on the horizons'.

Name: Isis

Role: Wife of Osiris, mother of Horus, goddess of women

Origin: Philae

Name: Khnum

Role: Ram god who created humans on the potter's wheel

Origin: Elephantine (first cataract of the River Nile)

Name: Khonsu

Role: Moon god

Origin: Karnak

Name: Meretseger

Role: Cobra goddess of the peak above the Valley of the Kings

Origin: Thebes

Name: Min

Role: God of fertility

Origin: Coptos/Akhmim

Name: Mut

Role: Lionness goddess, bringer of disease

Origin: Thebes

Name: Neith

Role: Goddess of the hunt, goddess of the dead, supreme creator goddess in Sais

Origin: Lower Egypt – Sais (western Delta)

Name: Nekhbet

Role: Vulture goddess

Origin: Upper Egypt – el-Kab

Name: Nephthys

Role: Goddess of the dead

Origin: Heliopolis

Name: Nut

Role: Sky goddess – mother of the Sun, Moon and heavenly bodies. Also goddess of death and burial

Origin: Heliopolis

Name: Osiris

Role: Symbol of eternal life. God of death, resurrection, fertility

Origin: Abydos and Busiris (central Delta)

Name: Ptah

Role: Creator god

Origin: Memphis

Name: Re/Ra/Ra-Amon

Role: Sun god

Origin: Heliopolis

Name: Sekhmet

Role: Lionness goddess of war and disease. Goddess of the sun's rays at midday

Origin: Memphis

Name: Seth

Role: God of the desert, god of foreign lands

Origin: Heliopolis

Name: Shu

Role: God of dry air, bearer of Heaven

Origin: Heliopolis

Name: Sobek

Role: Crocodile god. Creator God (as Sobek-Re)

Origin: Faiyum/Ombos

Name: Thoth

Role: God of sacred writings and wisdom

Origin: Hermopolis

Name: Wadjet

Role: Cobra goddess

Origin: Lower Egypt

The Divine Kings and Pharaohs

In the early, pre-dynastic days of Ancient Egypt after *c.* 5500 BC, kings were automatically classed as gods. They retained this divine status until the advent of the Old Kingdom in *c.* 2686 BC when a new concept emerged, that of kings 'transformed' into gods. Heirs to the throne were not considered as divine, but simply as the children of the king. An heir remained mortal until the time came for him to succeed to the throne. He could not ascend the throne in this state, but the problem was solved by the belief that, at birth, royal heirs possessed a physical being and a 'ka', a creative life force or living spirit. A secret ritual was performed in the inner area of the temple which united the physical and spiritual aspects of a new king and so turned him into a god. From then on, the now divine king's word was law.

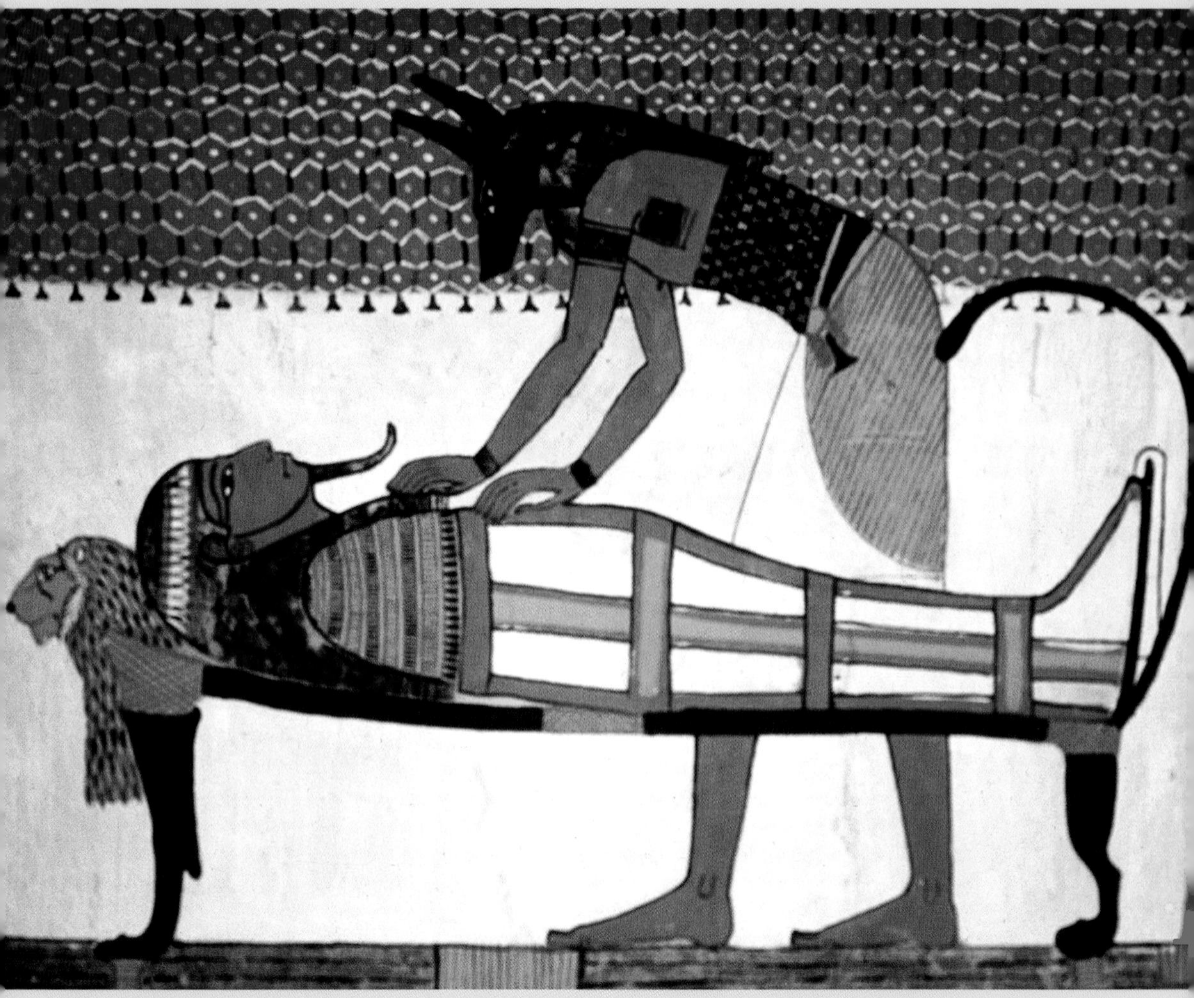

The Priests of Ancient Egypt

Priests were chosen by the king or inherited their post from a family member. The priesthood served two main functions: as temple officiants, and as administrators and bureaucrats running the temple estates. They controlled knowledge about the gods and access to the divine images when they appeared in the festivals; they interpreted the oracles that were delivered by the images, and made offerings on the behalf of worshippers. Most land in Egypt was owned by the state in the form of the palace and the temple: the temples therefore stored the produce of fields and distributed grain, bread, meat, other foodstuffs and linen as wages to the workers. They were, in a sense, the banks of Ancient Egypt.

Ancient Egyptian Creation Myths

The Egyptian view of creation took as its model the Nile flood. In the beginning, all was watery chaos, called Nun. In some versions of the creation, the 'primaeval hill' – the first land – emerged from this watery chaos, and the creator god, in the form of a falcon, alighted on it. In another version, a lotus bud grew up from the water, opening to reveal the new-born sun god. Elsewhere, the wild cow – Hathor – rose from the waters, and gave birth to the sun, which she then raised to the heavens between her horns.

Heliopolis

Atum came into existence by thought. Separated from the watery chaos, Nun, Atum then breathed, creating air (Shu); and spat, creating moisture (Tefnut), the ancestors of the other gods.

Memphis

At Memphis, the god Ptah, patron of all crafts, created the world by speaking.

Hermopolis

The inhabitants of Hermopolis, a city in Upper Egypt, worshipped the Ogdoad, a group of eight gods (four male-female pairs) who between them created the world and represented four concepts:

God and Goddess	Concept
Amun and Amunet	Hiddenness
Heh and Hauhet	Infinity
Kek and Kauket	Darkness
Nun and Nunet	Water/primordial ocean

Thebes

During the New Kingdom (1550–1069 BC), Amun of Thebes was merged with Ra the sun god of Heliopolis, and creation attributed to him in the form of a serpent: this was celebrated every week in the temple at Djeme, which represented the primaeval mound.

The Nature of the Egyptian Gods

Like the Ancient Greeks and Romans, the Egyptians saw their gods as essentially human by nature. Like humans, the gods were not immortal, but could die, like Osiris. Gods ate, drank, slept, loved, quarrelled, expressed emotion, hunted and fought battles and wars. Goddesses could conceive and give birth to children.

The Meaning of Dreams

The Egyptians believed that dreams allowed them to communicate with the gods, and forecast the future. Discovering whether a dream was good or bad was a matter of interpretation but there were a number of standard readings available. An early thirteenth-century-BC papyrus discovered near the Ramesseum on the west bank of the Nile, and now kept in the British Museum, contains a list in which dreams are described, interpreted and classified as good or bad. If, for instance, an Egyptian dreamed that he was drinking warm beer, this was a bad sign and he was due to suffer because of it.

The Temple as the Centre of Creation

An Ancient Egyptian temple was much more than a place of worship. A god lived there and everything about it symbolized some aspect of religious belief. An Egyptian temple reflected the world at the moment it was created. The mud brick wall that separated it from the world outside symbolized the ocean that comprised the cosmos before the creation. The pylon or entrance gate, formed from two towers joined by a masonry bridge, stood for the hieroglyph that represented the horizon. Temples were always orientated from east to west so that the rays of the rising sun passed through the pylon and into the shrine where a statue of the god stood. The rituals that took place in the temple traced the god's daily life – washing, anointing, adorning, dressing, feeding – and the festivals, when he either visited another deity or was visited by him, representated the two gods socializing.

The Rituals of the Temple

The king or pharaoh of Egypt was, when present, the high priest in the important temples of his realm and the protagonist in the rituals that were held there. Every day, at dawn, midday and in the evening, a service of purification was performed and offerings were placed before the temple god.

Festivals of Ancient Egypt

Ordinary Egyptians were forbidden to enter the inner areas of temples where the ruler and his priests performed the sacred rituals. To see their god, who was normally hidden away within his temple, the people had to wait for one or other of the religious festivals when the divine image was taken in procession from one temple to another. Fortunately for them, festivals were frequent in Ancient Egypt. There were 54 festivals listed in the Festival Hall of Thutmose III (1479–1425 BC) at Karnak and 60 in the mortuary temple of Ramesses III (1184–1153 BC) at Medinet Habu. Two of the most important events, both held in Thebes, were the Festival of Opet in the second month of the inundation season and the Beautiful Festival of the Valley. The New Year festival was of comparable importance. So was the Festival of the Nile, when offerings of food were made at shrines.

Sacrifices to Ra

The sacrifices of goats and cattle that took place at the temple of the sun god Ra at Heliopolis were much more than religious rituals. They had another, rather more mundane, purpose – to provide food for those attending the sacrifices. Vast quantities of meat were distributed among the people as well as specially prepared bread, beer and cakes. Heliopolis was the 'capital' of Ra and the sacrifices that were made to him there took place at the foot of a tall stone obelisk, which the god was thought to inhabit once the rays of the sun touched the top.

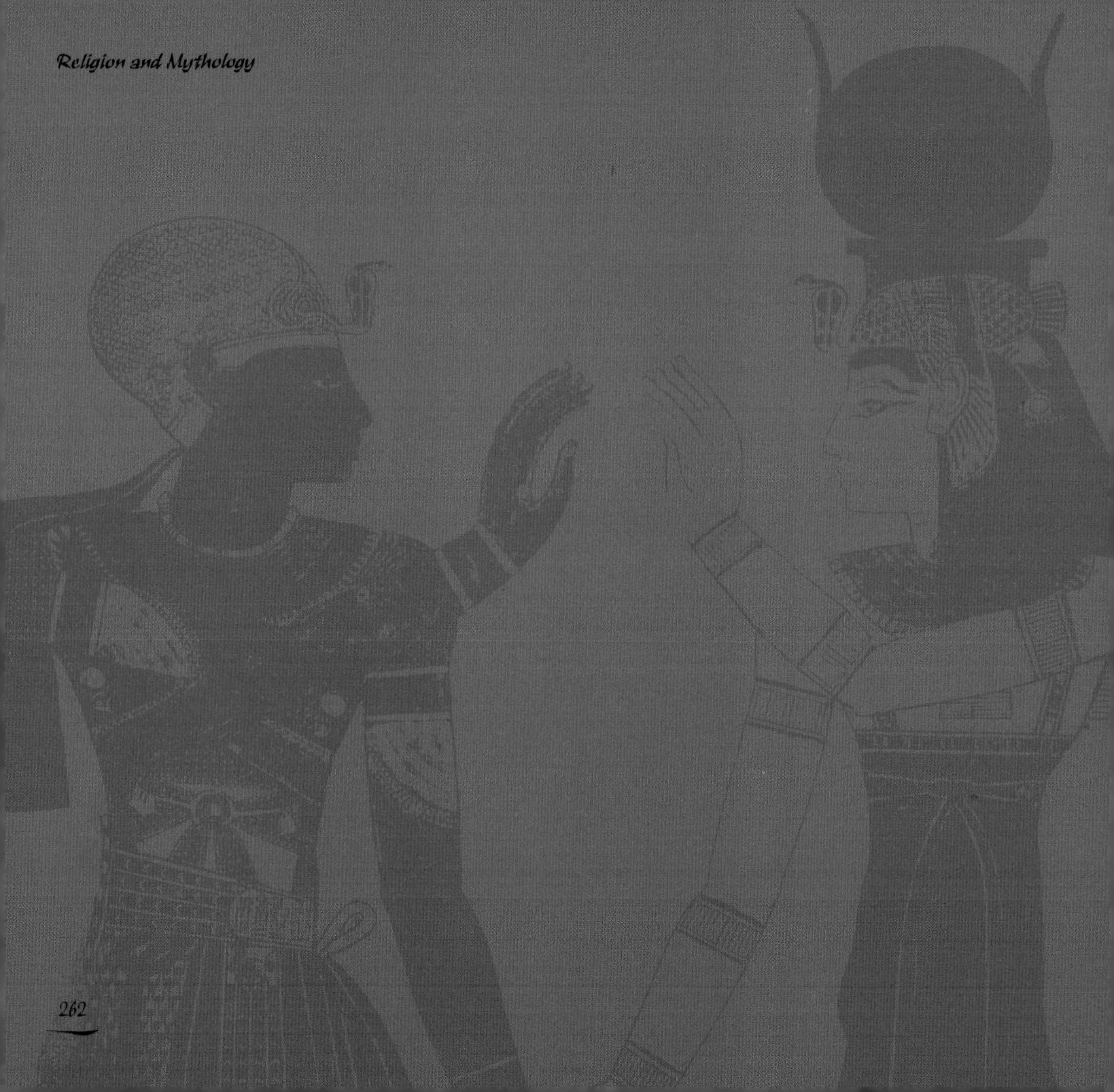

Oracles in Ancient Egyptian Religion

Religious festivals were often used as an occasion for consulting oracles. The practice first became prominent during the New Kingdom (1550–1069 BC) and pharaohs and high officials, as well as ordinary Egyptians, took advantage of it, possibly to demonstrate in public that their actions had divine approval. Questions put to the divine image during a festival were mainly concerned with health, family or property problems, and the priests carrying the bark shrine that contained the god only had to tilt it in one direction or the other to indicate a Yes or a No. In the later periods, petitions were frequently addressed to gods in temples and shrines, and also through dreams. Those seeking interpretation of their dreams could sleep in an area adjacent to the temple – as discovered when an archive of a dream interpreter was excavated in a large temple complex near the city of Memphis.

How do We know?

Although fragmentary, the data discovered by Egyptologists has provided a reasonably comprehensive picture of the spiritual life and thinking of the Ancient Egyptians. Hymns, spells, charms and prayers have been found inscribed on the walls of tombs and temples. They also appear on coffin lids, stelae, papyri, and statues. The earliest religious writings in Egypt were the Pyramid Texts dating from the Fifth (2494–2345 BC) and Sixth (2345–2181 BC) Dynasties. This was followed by other, similar books, including the *Book of the Dead*, containing 190 chapters, the *Book of the Gates* and the *Book of the Day and Night*. All were concerned with ensuring the welfare of the dead and a safe journey into the afterlife by means of spells, prayers, protective incantations and magical utterances. The texts, written on papyri, were placed inside coffins, incorporated into the bandages of mummies or inserted into statuettes of Sokar-Osiris, deities of the dead.

A Household of the Dead

Kings of the first two dynasties (3100–2686 BC) were not buried alone. Since death was regarded as a mirror image of life in Ancient Egypt, their graves needed to contain all they had known while alive. This included members of their household, their servants and their slaves. For example, 455 bodies were discovered when the tomb of King Wadji (*c.* 2980 BC) of the First Dynasty was excavated. Members of the king's personal household numbered 335. Also, the bodies of 77 female and 41 male important employees shared the grave of Wadji's queen, Merneith. Many of the servants buried with their employers were deliberately killed for the purpose, often by poison. Others were buried alive, to judge by the signs of panic at the prospect of suffocation that have been found during excavations. The positions of some of the bodies discovered by Egyptologists have revealed that frantic, though futile attempts to escape were made.

The Shabtis

After the first two dynasties kings were buried alone in their pyramids, with other tombs built around them. However, from the 11th Dynasty (2055–1985 BC), shabtis – statuettes 10–23 cm (4–9 in) high, made of wood, clay, stone, wax, terracotta, bronze, faience or glass – were substituted for the members of households formerly buried in the graves of kings. Apparently, even a king was not excused labour in the afterlife and the shabtis were meant to do the work for him. Chapter Six in the *Book of the Dead* contained the shabti's instructions: 'O shabti, if (name of the deceased) be summoned to do any work which has to be done in the realm of the dead, to make arable the fields, to irrigate the land or to convey sand from east to west, "Here am I" you shall say. "I shall do it." ' Some shabtis were dressed as farm or field workers, carrying hoes, picks, seed bags and pots of water, others as soldiers or sailors. The use of shabtis came to an end after 332 BC.

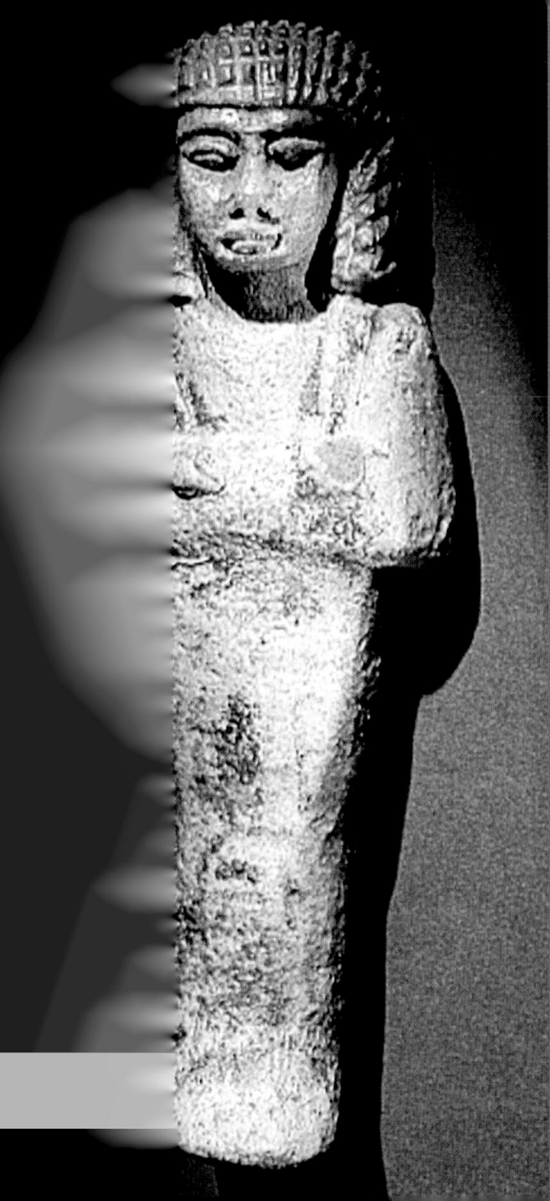

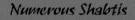

Numerous Shabtis

Over time, the numbers of shabtis deposited in tombs vastly increased, from one per grave to hundreds. There were some 700 shabtis in the tomb of the 19th-Dynasty King Sety I (1294–1279 BC), but this was exceeded by the 25th-Dynasty monarch Taharqa (690–664 BC), who was buried with over 1,000 shabtis.

The Religious Significance of Animals

The Apis Bull

In Ancient Egypt, all animals were regarded as holy and each of them was the incarnation on Earth of a god. None, though, was more sacred than the Apis Bull. The Apis was recognized by certain physical characteristics. It had to be black with a white triangle on its forehead, carry a vulture shape on its back, have double hairs on its tail and underneath its tongue show a mark in the shape of a scarab. While alive, the Apis Bull was considered to be the manifestation of Ptah, the creator god of Memphis. After death, it was identified with Osiris. When an Apis Bull died, it was embalmed and buried with its own shabtis. These took the form of miniature bulls which served the dead animal in the same way as their human counterparts. The death of an Apis Bull was the occasion for national mourning throughout Egypt.

Animals for Sacrifice

Although animals were considered holy in Ancient Egypt, this did not prevent their being used as sacrifices to the gods. The tests applied by priests in order to choose the most suitable animals were described by the Greek writer Herodotus. 'Male kine are tested in the following manner,' Herodotus wrote. 'One of the priests searches to see if there is a single black hair on the whole body, since in that case, the beast is unclean. He examines him all over after which he takes the tongue out of his mouth to see if it be clean in respect of the prescribed marks... '. If the animal passed these tests, 'the priest would twist a piece of papyrus round its horns and attach thereto some sealing clay, which he then stamps with his own signet ring. It is forbidden, under penalty of death, to sacrifice an animal which has not been marked in this way.'

Taboos in Ancient Egypt

Ancient Egyptian society was about divinely established order, and things that might upset that were bad – or *bwt* – what we might term 'taboo'. These might vary according to local cults. For example, fish, pork, or honey might be forbidden in some districts but not others. Uncircumcised men were also *bwt*. A triumphal stele erected by Piy (747–716 BC), Nubian founder of the 25th Dynasty, stated that the princes of Lower Egypt he had defeated were 'forbidden to enter the palace because they had not been circumcised and they were eaters of fish, which is an abomination to the palace, but King Nimlot (of Ashmunein in Upper Egypt) was able to enter ... because he was clean and did not eat fish.' In religious practices, the head of an animal could not be sacrificed because it was considered unclean and cursed. Nor could sheep be used. It was strictly forbidden to sacrifice a ewe because they were sacred to the goddess Isis.

Prayer to Amun

A prayer to Amun on offerings made during festivals reads thus:

'Lord of the Two Lands (of Upper and Lower Egypt),
King of Eternity, lord of everlastingness, may they
(worshippers at the festival) give you a thousand of
bread, beer, beef and fowl, a thousand of food offerings,
a thousand of drink offerings.'

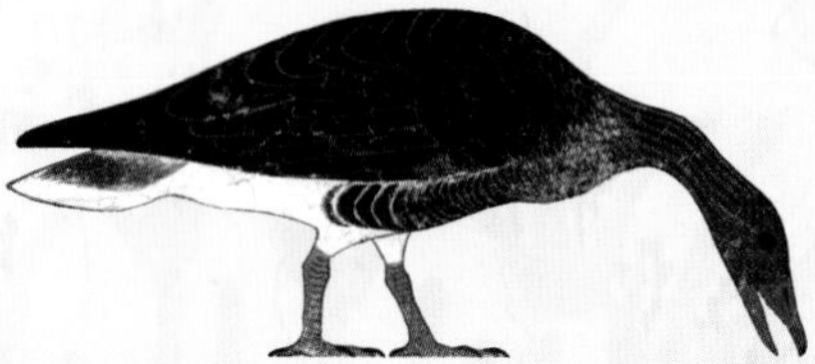

One of the Oldest in the World: Language and Communication

Ancient Egyptian

The Ancient Egyptian language has affinities with other African languages of north-east Africa and with Semitic languages of western Asia. It was one of the first written languages, the other being Sumerian. The earliest examples of both Egyptian and Sumerian script belong to the Fourth Millennium BC. By 3000 BC both were complex written languages, used mainly for economic texts.

The earliest written form of the Egyptian language was hieroglyphic – which began as simple depictions of things, but developed into a complex combination of signs, some representing things, and others standing for sounds. Some signs represent one sound ('r', 't', 'k'), others two ('mn', 'pt') or even three ('htp'). But, like modern Arabic and Hebrew, there are no true vowel sounds, so what is written is actually a skeleton of the spoken language. This means that many of the subtleties of the language are lost to us.

Development

Language	Date when in use	Historical Periods
Archaic Egyptian	Before 2600 BC	Early Dynastic; Old Kingdom
Old Egyptian	2600–2000 BC	Old Kingdom; 7th–10th Dynasties of First Intermediate Period
Middle Egyptian	2000–1300 BC	11th Dynasty of First Intermediate Period; Middle Kingdom; Second Intermediate Period; 18th Dynasty of New Kingdom
Late Egyptian	1300–700 BC	19th and 20th Dynasties of New Kingdom; 21st and 22nd Dynasties of the Third Intermediate Period
Demotic	700 BC–400s AD	23rd and 24th Dynasties of the Third Intermediate Period, Late Period and after

Literature

The range of subjects covered by Ancient Egyptian literature was vast. Religious texts included hymns to the gods, treatises on magic and mythology and funerary texts such as the *Book of the Dead*, which dated from the end of the Second Intermediate Period (1650–1550 BC) and contained some 200 spells or 'chapters', including the dramatic Chapter 125, detailing the last judgment of Osiris. The *Book of the Dead* had in turn derived its contents from the earliest Pyramid Texts dating from the latter years of the Old Kingdom (2375–2181 BC). Despite the intensely religious ethos of Ancient Egypt, there was also a huge range of secular literature – fiction, poems, 'biographies', histories and scientific, mathematical and medical texts. This category also includes the so-called 'wisdom' texts, which give advice on how to lead a respectable and successful life, how to behave in social situations, deal kindly with other people, even under provocation, and generally how to excel.

Genres of Ancient Egyptian Literature

These contrasting types of literature appeared during differing periods of Ancient Egyptian history. For instance, during the Old Kingdom (2686–2181 BC) most literature took the form of religious funerary texts or inscriptions on private tombs which eulogized the deceased person in poetic terms. During the Middle Kingdom (2055–1650 BC), literature became more light-hearted, exemplified by texts such as *The Tale of the Shipwrecked Sailor* or *The Tale of Sinuhe*. These stories were, purportedly, historical, but because of their entertaining plots and fantasy content, they have been classed as fiction. During the New Kingdom (1550–1069 BC) literary genres from the earlier kingdoms were enlarged and included specialized categories, such as annals, mathematical texts, king lists, decrees and treaties. The New Kingdom also saw the emergence of a new 'miscellaneous' genre – collections of hymns or prayers and personal accounts, including love poems containing dramatic monologues.

Advice from the Wisdom Texts

'Be skilful in speech, that you may be strong ... the tongue and words are braver than all fighting.'

'If you find a disputant arguing, a humble man who is not your equal, do not be aggressive against him ... let him alone that he may confute himself. Do not question him in order to relieve your feelings, do not vent yourself against your opponent, for wretched is he who would destroy him who is poor of understanding.'

'Acquire a good character without transgressing, for laziness on the part of the wise man does not happen.'

'Something else of value in the heart of God is to stop and think before speaking. ... The hot-headed man ... may you be restrained before him. Leave him to himself and God will know how to answer him.'

'Reprove yourself in your own eyes, take care that another man does not reprove you.'

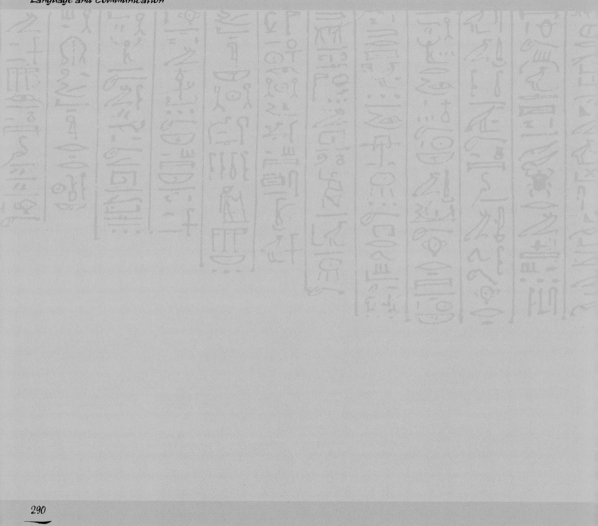

Tales of Gods and Magic

There are many stories surviving from Ancient Egypt, most probably deriving from oral literature. They often include gods and pharaohs, and frequently magic. In one collection of tales set in the golden age of the Pharaoh Sneferu (2613–2578 BC) the king's boating trip on his pleasure lake comes to a halt when one of the girls rowing him loses her turquoise hair ornament: the king's magician parts the waters so that she can retrieve it and the trip continues. One lengthy cycle of stories concerned the murder of Osiris; the search by his wife, Isis, for the body and its brief restoration to life, and the conflicts between Osiris's son, Horus, and his uncle Seth for the throne of Egypt. Some ancient Egyptian stories have similarities with those that later appear in the '*Arabian Nights*', many of which were written down in medieval Egypt.

The Tale of the Shipwrecked Sailor

A story dating back to the Middle Kingdom (2055–1650 BC) bears strong similarities to *Robinson Crusoe* written in 1719–20 by Daniel Defoe, except for its ending. *The Shipwrecked Sailor* is the story of an Egyptian sailor who is shipwrecked on an isolated island, with the rest of the crew having drowned. He survives alone for some time, and while exploring the island, he discovers treasure. He – and his treasure – are finally rescued and the sailor returns home. After he has departed, the island, having served its purpose, sinks beneath the sea and disappears.

Love Poetry

The romantic poetry of Ancient Egypt ran the gamut of expression from violent passion to delicate sentiment and affection. Egyptian poets were very fond of similes, and typically compared the object of their love to something beautiful and desirable. 'My beloved is like a garden, full of beautiful papyrus blossoms...' is one example. The fearlessness that went with intense love was expressed in 'My beloved is there on the other bank... On the bankside there is a crocodile lying in wait, but I am not afraid of it. I will swim through the water until I reach her and be delighted.'

Herodotus on Writing

In his *Histories*, the Greek writer Herodotus commented: 'When (the Egyptians) write or calculate, instead of going, like the Greeks, from left to right, they move their hand from right to left; and they insist, notwithstanding, that it is they who go to the right and the Greeks who go to the left.'

Papyrus

The papyrus reed, which grows in the freshwater marshes along the River Nile – though it is becoming fairly rare today, was a valuable multi-purpose material in Ancient Egypt. It served to make mattresses, mats, boxes, rope and baskets and was used in the construction of furniture. It was even possible to build small river boats out of papyrus. But its best-known use was as the material to which it gave its English name: paper.

To turn papyrus into paper, the outside of the 3 m- ($9^{3}/_{4}$ in)-tall plant was peeled away and sliced into thin strips. The sugar content was soaked off, then the papyrus was pounded to expel the water within. Another set of strips was placed at right angles to the first. After more pounding, the papyrus sheet was left under a heavy weight for six days. Rolls were made by gluing sheets of papyrus together: the longest were 20 sheets – up to 10.5 m ($34\ ^{1}/_{2}$ feet) long.

Papyrology

The first purchase of Ancient Egyptian papyri by a European dealer in antiquities took place in 1778 and with that, a new science, papyrology, was inaugurated. As more papyri were discovered or bought by archaeologists, European museums acquired collections from Memphis and Letopolis in Middle Egypt, and from Panopolis, Thebes, Hermonthis, Elephantine and Syene in Upper Egypt.

The first major discoveries of papyri occurred between 1820 and 1840, but there have been many other large finds, notably around 1900, when hundreds of thousands of papyrus fragments were recovered from the sites of Tebtunis and Oxyrhynchus. These are still being conserved and studied. Once reconstructed, deciphered and transcribed by papyrologists, they yielded a treasure house of information. This included examples of Ancient Egyptian literature, religious, magical and medical texts as well as the more mundane tax receipts and accounts, court documents and official letters of Ancient Egyptian bureaucracy.

Hieroglyphs

Hieroglyphic script, which is largely pictorial, was the most ancient form of Ancient Egyptian writing and made its first known appearance on pottery and labels in around 3100 BC, at the start of the Early Dynastic Period. The term for 'hieroglyph' in the Ancient Egyptian language was *mdju netjer*, meaning 'words of the gods'. Initially, hieroglyphs were the main form of writing used, but they were mostly consigned to religious purposes once the hieratic script evolved after *c.* 2686 BC. Stone monuments and temples were emblazoned with inscribed hieroglyphs. The Greeks called them *hiera grammata*, 'sacred letters', or *ta hieroglyphica*, 'sacred carved letters'.

Reading Hieroglyphs

Hieroglyphs are pictures (ideograms) of things: they may be whole, or parts of, animals, humans, plants, objects, tools, or weapons. These pictures were originally used to designate the 'thing' itself. So 'a man' was written with a seated figure of a man. Many signs were also used as sound values (phonograms): so the hieroglyph of a door-bolt was used for the sound 's'.

As writing developed, combinations of picture and sound signs were used. The word for man was *s* (probably pronouned 'es'), so was written with the door-bolt hieroglyph, followed by the man hieroglyph; 'woman' was *st* (pronounced 'eset' – *t* is the feminine ending), so would be written with the door bolt, plus *t* (a loaf of bread) and the woman hieroglyph. These hieroglyphs were put after a name to indicate the sex.

Writing Hieroglyphs

Hieroglyphs could be written in three different ways. Some inscriptions ran horizontally from right to left, others from left to right. Hieroglyphs were also carved vertically, in columns, facing left-to-right or right-to-left, and were read from top to bottom. This versatility meant that hieroglyphics were extremely decorative and could be used in symmetrical horizontal and vertical inscriptions around doorways. It also allowed lines or columns of text to be included to give captions to scenes, naming the gods and people, and the actions involved. There was even greater importance to this ability to orientate the script. In temples, the gods are generally shown as if emerging from the innermost rooms and the king and other figures as if entering, the captions are therefore oriented to the appropriate figures, and the two sides of the temple have symmetry.

Hieratic Script

Writing hieroglyphs required artistry, it was a task to be carried out with painstaking care and delicacy. As such, it was not particularly suitable for business or administrative use. This was why the cursive hieratic script developed as a faster method of writing, with simpler signs that could quickly record information. It was originally used in everything from literary to scientific documents, but religious too – in fact, the Greeks gave it the name 'hieratic' after they saw it used exclusively by Ancient Egyptian priests (*hieratikos* in Greek meant 'priestly'). The earliest hieratic texts so far excavated date from the Fourth Dynasty (2613–2494 BC) and comprise records of estates.

Demotic Script

Demotic, another cursive script also named by the Greeks, meant 'popular writing' or 'writing commonly used' and was derived from hieratic. But by the 26th Dynasty of the Late Period (664–525 BC) it had replaced its predecessor except for funerary and religious purposes. Initially, demotic was used for bureaucratic and commercial writing, but after 332 BC, and the advent of the Macedonian dynasty of Ptolomaic pharaohs, it was used more widely, for scientific, literary, technical and even religious texts. The script proved very versatile, suited to inscriptions on monuments and stelae. It was one of the three scripts inscribed on the Rosetta Stone.

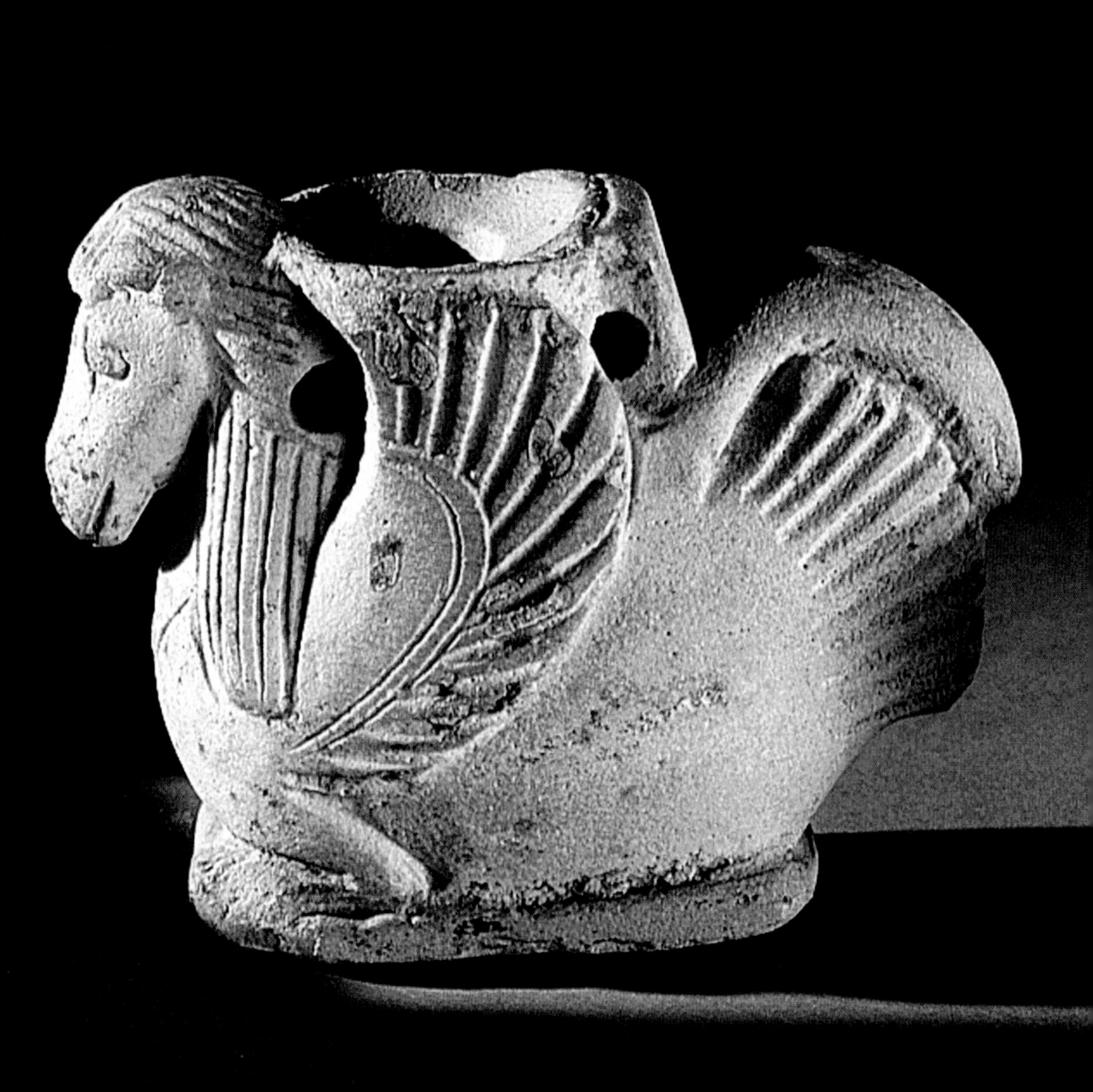

Honorific Transposition

The need to demonstrate respect and awe for the gods and their incarnations, the pharaohs, was absolute in Ancient Egypt and forms of writing were manipulated to make sure this was observed. The method used by scribes was called 'honorific transposition'. This involved placing the sign representing a god or the name of a god, goddess or pharaoh first, before any other sign in a sentence. If a sentence referred to both a god or goddess and a pharaoh too, the pharaoh took second place.

Scribes and their Tools

Appropriately enough, the hieroglyph for 'scribe' and 'writing' depicted the tools of the scribe. There was his wooden or stone palette which contained two blocks of ink, usually red and black. Ink was made from soot or the pigment red ochre, or by crushing brightly coloured minerals or plants and adding water. Scribes also carried a water pot, leather bag and a set of reed brushes. They wrote on a variety of different surfaces – papyrus of course, but also chips of stone and potsherds called 'ostraca', sheets of leather and wooden boards thinly covered in plaster.

Whether they ended their careers as priests, civil servants, architects, or army generals, all members of the ruling class began by training as scribes. In ancient Egypt, writing meant power. The 'scribes' ruled the country, and access to the temple and palace schools was strictly controlled.

Thoth, God of Writing and Scribes

As well as his function as god of sacred writings and wisdom, Thoth was patron of scribes. In the temple of Ramesses II at Abydos, a relief sculpture shows Thoth seated on his throne with a long scribe's palette in one hand and a reed for writing in the other.

Ahmes the Scribe

Ahmes (1680–1620 BC) who wrote the 'Rhind' Papyrus (*see* page 343) was a modest man. He took no credit for the papyrus, protesting that he was 'merely' the scribe. But Ahmes was meticulous about 'accurate reckoning' which, he said, was 'the entrance into the knowledge of all existing things and all obscure secrets.'

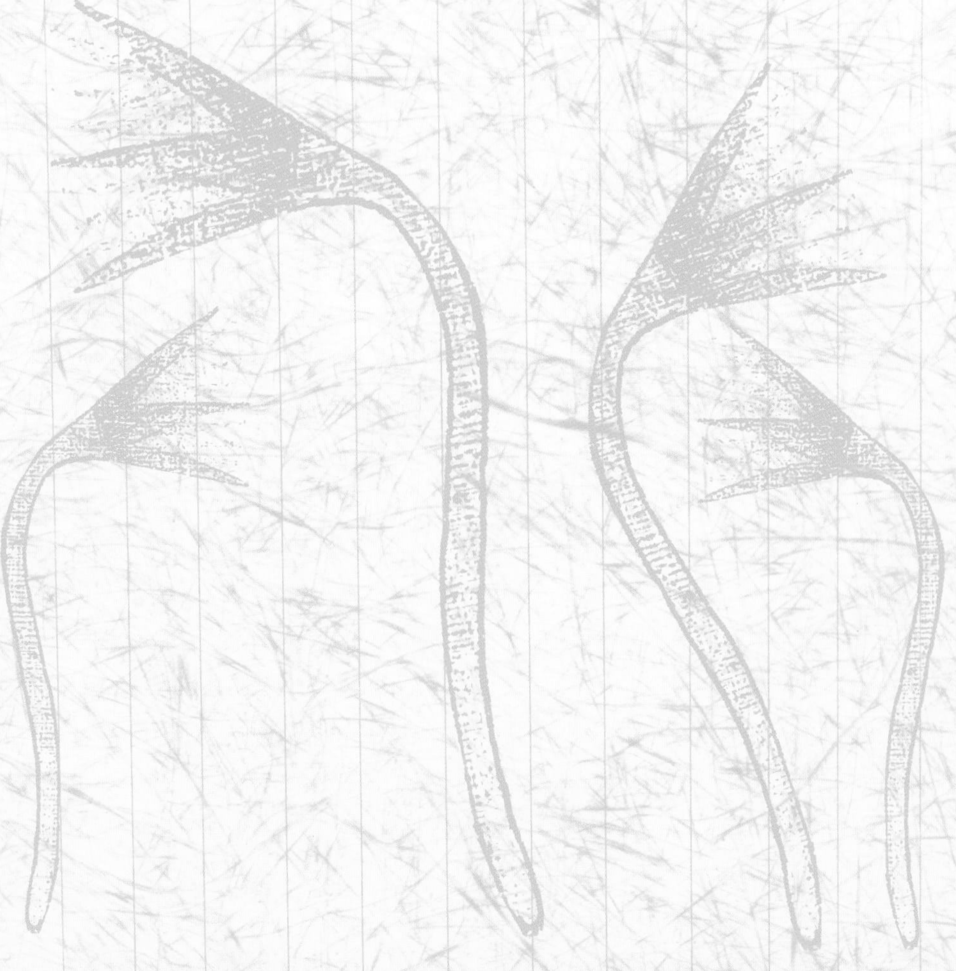

The Scribe Statue

A popular artefact in Ancient Egypt was the Scribe Statue, showing a scribe in their traditional cross-legged pose, which came to be symbolic of their high status.

Scribal Schools

Egyptians viewed the ability to write as a form of immortality, for a scribe's work outlived him and transmitted his knowledge to subsequent generations. One scribe remarked that the names of scribes 'are still preserved because of their books... and their memory lasts to the limits of eternity.' The scribal schools were normally attached to a temple or palace and the education was rigorous: to write scientific, medical, magical and other specialized texts, scribes had to understand the subjects involved. The curriculum included astronomy, geography, mathematics, law, the interpretation of dreams and theology. In British excavations at el-Amarna (Akhetaten) between 1921 and 1926, one building was discovered which had its bricks stamped with the words 'Per Ankh' – House of Life. The 'House of Life' was the place where scribes copied books – thus preserving old literature – and compiled new works. These books were then placed in the 'House of Books', the Library, attached to all of the main temples of Egypt.

Learning to Write

Apprentice scribes came from the ruling families and started training at an early age. They were sent to the House of Life sometimes as young as six and underwent several years of formal education. Privileged status did not excuse them from long hours of work, or protect them from strict teachers and their punishments for inattention or missing class – bad behaviour was rewarded with a good beating from the teacher's stick. Young scribes were not allowed to use papyrus, which was expensive, but instead wrote on pieces of broken clay pottery or flakes of stone. Their teachers dictated stories or moral tracts which the boys wrote down. The boys also copied passages from the *Book of Kemyt*, which contained special exercises teaching them how to form hieroglyphics clearly. Once the trainees graduated and started work, they went on copying, but this time from works of literature, poetry and panegyrics.

Writing and Magic

Religion and magic were integral to the mindset of Ancient Egyptians, and hieroglyphs played their part in furthering the constant quest for protection against evil. The hieroglyph representing a scorpion was drawn without the scorpion's deadly tail to protect against its poisonous sting, and the hieroglyphs denoting Apophis, the sinister snake-god of the underworld and the representative of the forces of evil and chaos, depicted a snake stabbed or cut about in order to repel the deity's innate wickedness. Another way of eluding evil in writing was to omit or strike out the name of an enemy, a demon or an evil god. This was why the names of the renegade pharaoh Akhenaten, his relatives and Aten, the Sun-god he promoted, were mostly obliterated from walls, monuments and wherever else they had been inscribed. Simply by removing a hated name, the Egyptians believed they were harming the person to whom it belonged.

Maths to Magic: Science and Technology

Science in Ancient Egypt

Science as it is understood today did not characterize Ancient Egyptian society. Their 'science' did not involve pure research or the formulation of general scientific or mathematical principles, but the need to use practical skills for practical purposes. There was, in fact, no particular word for 'science' in the language of Ancient Egypt. Egyptian 'scientists' were concerned with how to shift very heavy stones, calculate the height of pyramids or work out angles involved in architectural construction. When seeking explanations, the tendency was to ascribe phenomena to divine will. It appears, too, that the Egyptians never sought to discover why a six-hour shortfall in the year made for incongruity between the calendar and the seasons. Even so, some practices later labelled 'scientific' existed in Ancient Egypt. The Egyptians were familiar with 'scientific' procedures such as keeping records, making astronomical observations or deducing the cause of disease from observing a patient's symptoms.

Mathematics

Mathematics was extremely important for a complex civilization like Ancient Egypt, with its reliance on engineering, sophisticated architecture, astronomy and the administrative need to keep meticulous records of population, taxes and crop yields and storage.

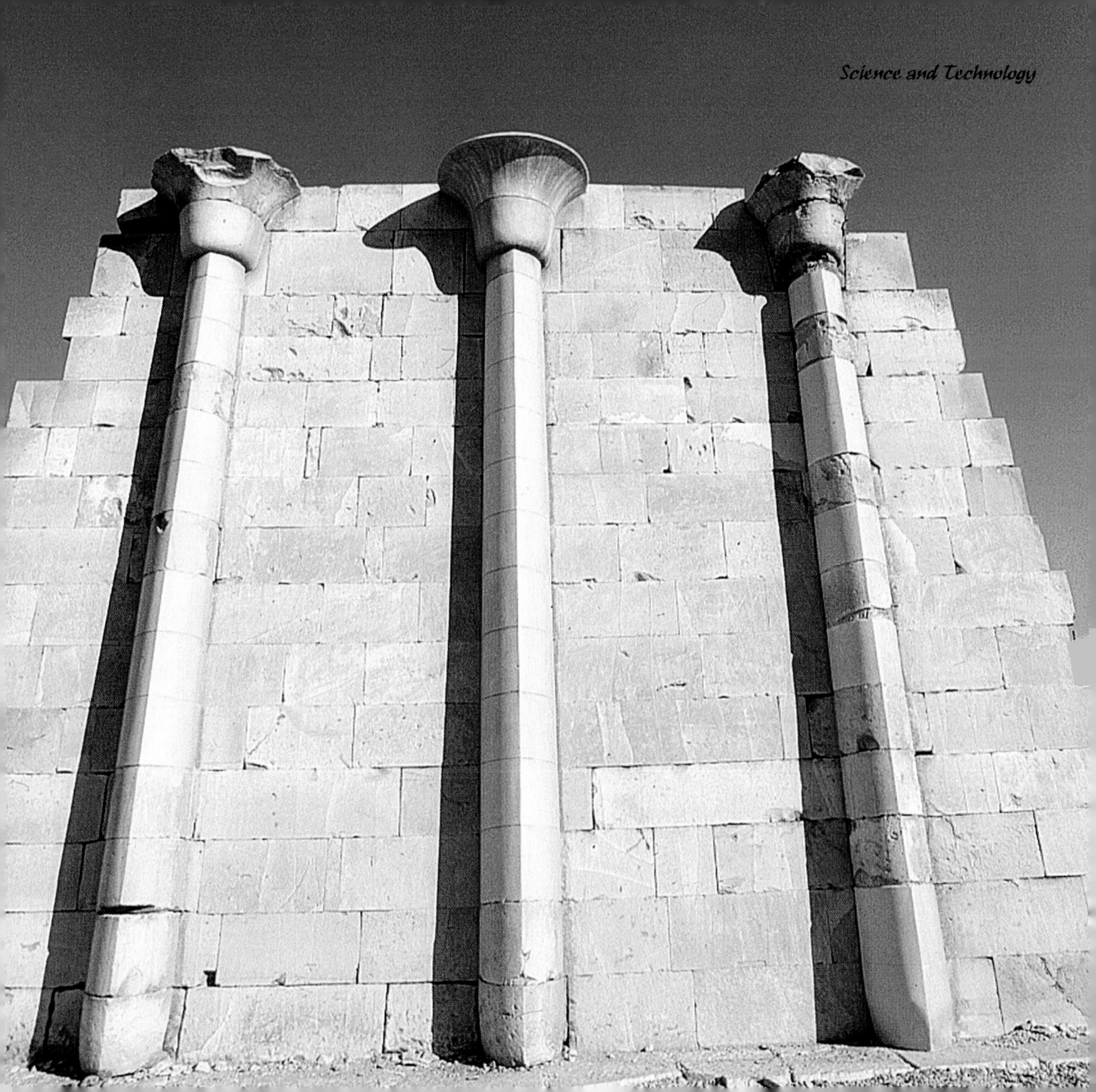

The Egyptian Numbers System

Ancient Egyptian mathematics was decimal, but used the 'add up' system. Six of its seven symbols were pictographic. The exception was the figure '1', which took the form of a single stroke repeated twice for two and so on down to nine.

Single symbols were used for larger figures up to one million. A drawing of a cattle hob was used for 10, a coiled rope for 100, a lotus flower for 1,000, a finger for 10,000, a frog, toad or tadpole for 100,000 and a god with arms uplifted for one million. The raised arms have sometimes been taken as a sign of desperation, since the gesture has been translated as 'more than I can count.'

Multiplying and Dividing

Multiplying by 10 involved changing pictograms, for instance in 100 x 10, by substituting the symbol for 100 with the symbol for 1,000. Multiplying other numbers, such as 19 x 13, combined doubling and 'add up'. First, the number one was doubled to two, two to four and twice more to reach 16. Next, the figure 19 was reached by adding one + two + 16. After this, these three figures were multiplied by 13 and added together, i.e. one x 13 = 13; plus two x 13 = 26; plus 16 x 13 = 208: giving the final total of 247. When dividing numbers, this process was reversed.

Geometry

Geometrical skills were essential for the accurate construction of official buildings, temples and pyramid tomb complexes. Some theories have ascribed the precision and symmetry of these complexes to mystical purposes. The evidence found on Ancient Egyptian monuments tells a more pragmatic story, showing how Egyptian engineers were mainly concerned with practical mathematics and geometry. They knew, for instance, that a triangle drawn inside a rectangle where the length and height of each shape were the same, had an area that was half that of the rectangle. The Egyptians were also able to calculate the area of a circle and the volume of a cylinder and pyramid.

Measurements

Ancient Egyptian bureaucracy was served by a wide variety of instruments including measures for recording the amounts of agricultural produce that were assessed for taxation purposes once every two years. The chief unit of measurement was the royal cubit (52.4 cm / $20\frac{2}{3}$ in). Land surveyors used the double *remen* which was divided into 40 units of 1.85 cm ($\frac{3}{4}$ in) each and the *meh-ta* of 100 royal cubits. The *setjat* or the *aroura* of 100 square cubits was used to measure area. Among measures of capacity were the *hekat* (4.77 litres / 10 pints) and the *hin* which was one 10th of a *hekat* and could be subdivided into units as small as one 32nd.

Ahmes and the Rhind Papyrus

The Egyptian scribe Ahmes (1680–1620 BC) wrote the 'Rhind' Papyrus, one of the oldest mathematical documents in the world. Named after the British antiquarian Alexander Rhind (1833–63) who acquired it in 1858, the papyrus derived its information from another document of *c.* 2650 BC and contains problems in mathematics, geometry and algebra and their solutions.

The Nilometer

The annual inundation of the Nile which fertilized the river banks and adjacent fields was of vital importance to the survival of Ancient Egypt. A nilometer, one design of which featured a series of steps down into the water with depth markings at intervals, was used to check on river levels and records were kept of the maximum height which the flooding reached.

Astronomy and Astrology

Both astrology, and later astronomy, were studied from the earliest times in Ancient Egypt. A prime astrological concern was the significance of heavenly bodies in religion and its rituals. And the scientific knowledge acquired from astronomy enabled the development of calendars, time calculation and the use of such data in the alignment of buildings.

Astrological and astronomical images proliferated on the ceilings of temples, the inside and outside of coffin lids and along the corridors and walls of pyramid tombs. The connection with religion was typified by the sky goddess Nut, whose body, studded with stars, was stretched over the Earth to protect it. Similarly, Nut protected mummies in their tombs by spreading herself over them. In this way, as the *Pyramid Texts* (funerary texts on the interior walls of some pyramids) put it, they might be 'placed among the imperishable stars'. During the Middle Kingdom (2055–1650 BC), Egyptian astronomers identified five planets of the solar system, but considered them to be gods sailing the heavens in barques.

Observing the Stars the Ancient Egyptian Way

The astronomer-priests of Ancient Egypt developed a simple, but effective way of observing the stars and their movements. Two priests would situate themselves on a north-south axis. One of the priests sat absolutely motionless while the other used him as a fixed point of reference to study the stars as they moved across the night sky. One instrument used for observations was the central rib of a palm leaf. Another, employed to study constellations of stars, was called *merkhet*, or 'instrument of knowing'. It was possible to deduce the time from these observations. The charts found painted on the ceilings of three 20th Dynasty tombs (1186–1069 BC) stated: 'When the star Orion is above the left eye (of the motionless priest) it is the seventh hour. When the star that follows Sothis (Sopdet, personification of Sirius) is above the left eye, it is the eighth hour.'

The Beaten Path of the Stars

The name Ancient Egyptian astronomers gave to the galaxy we now as the Milky Way was 'the beaten path of the stars'.

The Ancient Egyptian Zodiac

Although the signs of the zodiac as known today were introduced after 323 BC, when Alexander the Great assumed power in Ancient Egypt, the Egyptians already had an ancient zodiacal chart of their own. The 12 time periods were approximately the same in both zodiacs, although in the Egyptian they were represented by gods or spirits and the cycle began at the end of August, not in the Spring, as in the Greek zodiac.

The Signs of the Zodiac

Time period	Egyptian zodiac sign	Greek zodiac sign
29 August to 27 September	Thoth, god of learning	(Virgo)
28 September to 27 October	Horus, god of the sun	(Libra)
28 October to 26 November	Wadjet, goddess of the royal, cobra and symbol of knowledge	(Scorpio)
27 November to 26 December	Sekhmet, goddess of war	(Sagittarius)
27 December to 25 January	Sphinx, guardian of treasure	(Capricorn)
26 January to 24 February	Shu, god of sunlight and wind	(Aquarius)
25 February to 26 March	Isis, goddess of discipline	(Pisces)
27 March to 25 April	Osiris, god of the underworld	(Aries)
26 April to 25 May	Amun, creator of the world	(Taurus)
26 May to 24 June	Hathor, goddess of Earth and sky	(Gemini)
25 June to 24 July	Phoenix, bird of life and resurrection	(Cancer)
25 July to 28 August	Anubis, guardian of the underworld	(Leo)

The Ancient Egyptian Calendar

Ancient Egyptian calendars were initially based on the phases of the Moon and the yearly inundation of the River Nile, as measured by Nilometers (*see* page 344). The calendar was closely tied to the cycle of inundation (*akhet*), the first appearance of crops (*peret*) and harvest time (*shemu*). Each of the three seasons consisted of four months of 30 days each and each month of three weeks lasting 10 days each. Many hundreds of years later, this neat, simple arrangement was revived for a while at the time of the French Revolution of 1789. Day and night in Ancient Egypt each lasted 12 hours. The heliacal rising of the 'dog star' Sirius signalled the start of the Egyptian year which occurred on 30 July, according to the much later Gregorian Calendar in use today. Religious calendars also in use in Egypt reckoned festivals and ceremonies from the lunar month of 29.5 days.

The Months of the Ancient Egyptian Year

In Ancient Egypt, the months of the year did not acquire individual names until the New Kingdom (1550–1069 BC). Previously, as the table opposite shows, they were classified in thirds of a year by season. The individual names eventually evolved into the Hellenistic names still used by the Coptic Church today.

Month No.	Seasonal Name	Individual Name	Coptic Name
1	First of Akhet	Tekh	Thoth
2	Second of Akhet	Menhet	Phaophi
3	Third of Akhet	Hwt Hwr	Athyr
4	Fourth of Akhet	Ka-Hr-Ka	Khoiak
5	First of Peret	Sf-bdt	Tybi
6	Second of Peret	Rekh Wer	Mekhir
7	Third of Preret	Rekh Neds	Phamenoth
8	Fourth of Peret	Renwet	Pharmouthi
9	First of Shemu	Hnsw	Pakhon
10	Second of Shemu	Hnt-Htj	Payni
11	Third of Shemu	Ipt-Hmt	Epiphi
12	Fourth of Shemu	Wep-Renpet	Mesore

Lucky and Unlucky Days

In Ancient Egypt, lucky days were marked on calendars in black and the unlucky days in the warning colour, red.

Science and Technology

Farming

Farming in the area around the Nile was made relatively easy by the annual flooding of the river which richly fertilized the land. This does not mean, however, that there was no hard, back-breaking work involved. Ploughing, hoeing, harvesting and threshing still needed to be done. Egyptian farmers are thought to have been the first people to use a plough, which in their day took the form of a bow-shaped stick. This was dragged along the ground, sometimes with farm workers harnessed to it or later, by around 2000 BC, with oxen. After sowing seed, farmers drove sheep or pigs over the ground to tread it in. Sickles made of flint and wood were used to cut crops. Threshing crops like wheat was done by men wielding whips to get the kernels out of the husks. Afterwards, cattle or sheep were driven over the threshing floor to complete the task.

The Shaduf – A Tool from the Ancient Past

The *shaduf*, which is still used in some places along the banks of the Nile, is one of the most ancient agricultural implements in the world. First depicted on a cylinder seal from the ancient Mesopotamian city of Akkad some 5000 years ago, it was introduced into Eygpt during the 18th Dynasty (1550–1295 BC). Pictures of it were painted on the walls of tombs built in the 14th century BC. The purpose of the shaduf was to irrigate land by transferring water to channels close by a river or canal using a long wooden pole with a bucket at one end and a counterweight at the other.

Technology

Using Metals in Ancient Egypt

The skills of artisans were well developed early in Ancient Egyptian history and the working of copper, iron, gold and other metals reached a high level of expertise. The Egyptians mined copper in the desert between the Red Sea and the River Nile and as early as 3400 BC had acquired a keen understanding of how to extract the metal from ores. They called iron *ba-en-pet*, 'the metal of Heaven', since the first supplies of this metal came from meteorites. Much stronger and harder than copper, iron was very suitable for making tools and by around 666 BC, the Egyptians were able to case-harden the edges of their tools for greater cutting power and efficiency. As for gold, more than 100 ancient workings have been found in Egypt and the Sudan. Gold mining and working were very labour intensive, to judge by the 1,300 gold miners' houses built near the Red Sea coast that still survive today.

Glass-making in Ancient Egypt

Glass-making was already extant in Ancient Egypt during the 18th Dynasty (1550–1069 BC) when a ball bead, the oldest glass object so far found, was manufactured for the Pharaoh Amenhotep I (1525–1504 BC). After 1881, at Tell el-Amarna, the English Egyptologist Sir Flinders Petrie discovered glass furnaces that had once manufactured jars, beads, rods and figurines. These objects, which dated from 1400 BC, were made not by glass-blowing, which had not yet been devised, but by glass moulding. This involved making cores of clay, then covering them with glass and after firing, removing the cores. The Egyptians worked with coloured glass, which was often delicately patterned. Artificial glass 'pearls' were an important item of export and the vast quantity produced in Egypt gave rise to legends about enormous emeralds and other costly jewels, which were taken for the real thing but were more likely to have been made of glass paste.

Medicine and Magic

In Ancient Egypt, magic and medicine were inextricably linked. The most common remedies were amulets – small items in the form of gods, creatures or objects that were believed to exert healing or protective powers – and magic spells that were cast in search of a cure. This unscientific 'medicine' arose from the sincere belief that all illness was caused by malign influences or was divine punishment for bad behaviour.

There were specialists such as the surgeons known as Priests of the goddess Sekhmet (She who is Powerful), veterinary surgeons and dentists. One of the ancient medical papyri, the *Kahun*, dating from *c.* 2100–1900 BC, deals with female fertility and details a contraceptive made of crocodile excrement and sour milk. The Berlin papyrus of *c.* 1550 BC contains a pregnancy test which involves moistening barley and emmer with urine. If the barley grew, the child would be male, if the emmer grew, it would be female. If neither grew, there was no pregnancy.

Magic Bricks

During the New Kingdom (1550–1069 BC), magic bricks were placed in tombs, one on each of the four sides. Made of mud, they were meant to preserve the dead person from evil influences. Each brick contained a protective amulet, and was inscribed with quotations from the *Book of the Dead*.

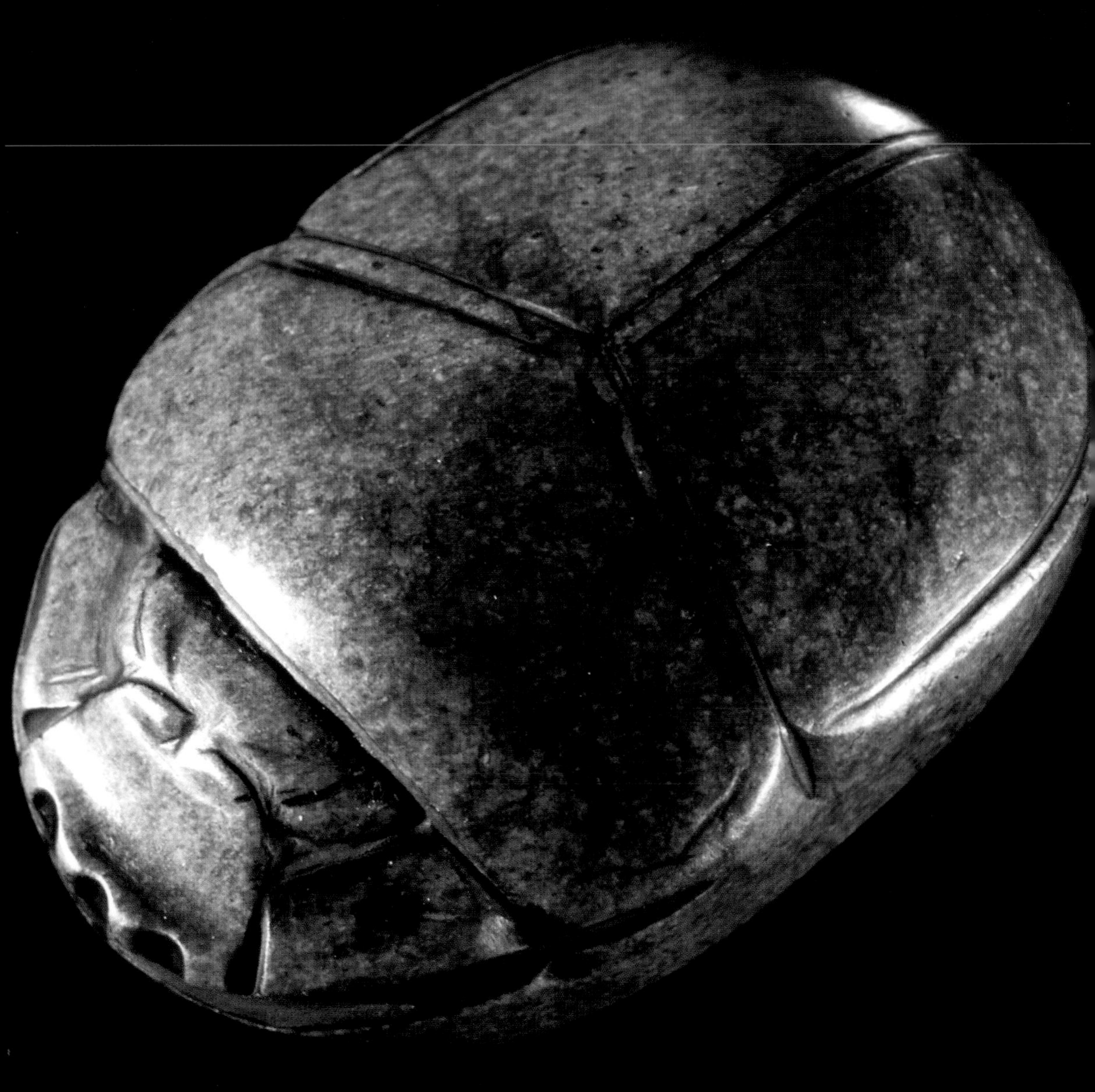

Casting Spells in Ancient Egypt

Ancient Egypt was a culture permeated by religious belief. Magic, amulets, charms and incantations frequently served as protection from evil. Spells were also important in relation to tombs where they were written or inscribed on paintings, statues or grave goods. Spells were meant to ensure that the deceased could live on after death.

Medicine and Magic Fail to Save Vizier

When the vizier Washptah, collapsed in front of the Pharaoh Neferirkare (2475–2455 BC), the pharaoh called for books of magic and medicine and ordered spells cast to save him. As the inscription of Washptah's tomb reveals, all efforts failed, but as archaeologists later discovered, many magical books were still buried with him.

How to Mummify a Corpse

In Ancient Egypt, it was imperative that a corpse should be preserved so that it could live again in the afterlife. This was the purpose of mummification or embalming, a practice dating back to the Old Kingdom (2686–2181 BC). Mummification ensured the body would not decay and that its *ka* or life force could still inhabit it. In around 450 BC, the Greek historian Herodotus described the 'best' and most expensive embalming method:

'First of all,' wrote Herodotus, 'they draw out the brains through the nostrils with an iron hook... Next they make an incision in the flank ...through which they extract all the internal organs. They then clean out the body cavity ... and stitch it up again.' Afterwards, 'they cover the corpse with natron for 70 days... and so mummify it. They wash the corpse and wrap it from head to toe in bandages of the finest linen anointed with gum'.

The Eye of Horus

The Eye of Horus, or the *wadjet* eye (menaing 'whole'), was an extremely powerful symbol of protection. Amulets containing the Eye of Horus were entombed with Egyptian pharaohs and were frequently placed over the spot where incisions were made in the process of embalming the corpse. Spiritually at least, the amulet was supposed to heal the incision and so make the Pharaoh whole once again.

The eyes of Horus not only possessed powerful magic, but between them embraced the entire universe. Additionally, the right eye symbolized the sun, male strength, mathematics and logic, while the left, also known as the Eye of Thoth, represented magic and creativity.

Time

Star Clocks in the Night Sky

On Ancient Egyptian star charts, such as those painted on temple ceilings, the night sky was divided into 36 groups of stars or 'decans'. Every year, for a period of 10 days, each decan rose above the horizon at dawn. Sirius, the Dog Star, the brightest of all, was of special importance since its rising coincided with the yearly inundation of the River Nile. This was why the rising of Sirius signalled the start of the Ancient Egyptian new year. Once the 10 days were over, another 'guardian' star rose above the horizon at dawn. It lasted another 10 days in its turn, before being replaced. Each decan was personified by a god or goddess. The goddess Sopdet, for example, was the guardian deity of Sirius. Her mythical consort Sah represented the constellation of Orion. Once its 10-day period was over, each decan spent 70 days in the Underworld.

Clepsydra

The *clepsydra* was a water-clock in which water ran out through a hole in the base of a stone, pottery or copper jar. The earliest yet found dates from the 18th Dynasty (1550–1295 BC). The passage of time was indicated by the amount of water remaining – measured via markings on the vessel or on a rod inserted into the water.

Picture Credits

All pictures courtesy of Werner Forman Archive, and the creative manipulation of Lucy Robins.

Some pictures courtesy of Werner Forman Archive and the following:
Ariadne Gallery, New York: 122–23, 203; Ashmolean Museum, Oxford: 36–37, 41, 134–35, 303; British Museum, London: 18–19, 110, 118–19, 140–41, 144, 161, 171, 197, 198, 206–7, 216, 218, 250, 290, 292–93, 307, 353, 366–67, 377; Collection of George Ortiz, Vandoeuvres: 50; Dr. E Strouhal: 16, 38–39, 60–61, 100, 106–7, 154, 188, 201, 209, 233, 238–39, 244–45, 253, 341, 327, 346–47, 356–57, 375; Egyptian Museum, Berlin: 156–57; Egyptian Museum, Cairo: 20–21, 29, 30, 42, 46, 59, 92–93, 96, 108–9, 120, 126, 143, 149, 162, 165, 172, 176, 184, 195, 211, 214–15, 222, 236–37, 242–43, 269, 277, 280–82, 294–95, 312–13, 314–15, 320–21, 343, 352, 368; Egyptian Museum, Turin: 349; Fitzwilliam Museum, Cambridge: 179, 226–27, 260–61, 316–17; John Klude Collection, Virginia: 186–87; Luxor Museum, Egypt 183; Metropolitan Museum of Art, New York: 139; Nederlandsches Museum van Oudheden te Leyden: 158; Private Collection, London: 152–53, 308; Royal Museum of Art & History, Brussels: 136; Schimmel Collection, New York: 150, 221; Schultz Collection, New York: 241; Sold at Christie's, London: 370–71; The Louvre Museum, Paris: 129, 257, 284, 286–87, 296, 311, 374.

Resources

Bibliography & Further Reading

Brunson, Margaret *Encyclopedia of Ancient Egypt*, (Facts on File Inc., 2002)
Budge, Sir E. Wallis *Book of the Dead: Hieroglyphic Transcript and Translation into English of the Papyrus of Ani* (Gramercy Book, 1995)
Clark, Rosemary *The Sacred Tradition in Ancient Egypt: The Esoteric Wisdom Revealed* (Llewellyn Publishers, 2000)
Gahlin, Lucia *The Myths and Mythology of Ancient Egypt* (Southwater, 2003)
Hoffman, Michael *Egypt before the Pharaohs: The Prehistoric Foundations of Egyptian Civilisation* (Barnes & Noble, 1994)
James, T.G.H. *An Introduction to Ancient Egypt* (Icon Editions, 1989)
James, T.G.H. *Exploring the World of the Pharaohs: Complete Guide to Ancient Egypt* (Thames & Hudson, 1990)
Lewis, Brenda Ralph *Ritual Sacrifice* (Sutton Publishing, 2001)
O'Connor, David B. *Ancient Egyptian Society (The Carnegie Series on Egypt)* (Premier Book Marketing Ltd., 1990)
Parkinson, R.B. *Voices from Ancient Egypt: An Anthology of Middle Kingdom Writings* (University of Oklahoma Press, 1991)
Ray, John *Reflections of Osiris: Lives from Ancient Egypt* (Oxford University Press, 2002)

Reeves, Nicholas (and Seventh Earl of Caernarvon) *The Complete Tutankhamun: The King, the Tomb, the Royal Treasure* (Thames & Hudson, 1995)
Rice, Michael *Who's Who in Ancient Egypt* (Routledge, 1999)
Rice, Michael *Egypt's Making: The Origins of Ancient Egypt 5000–2000 BC* (Routledge, 2003)
Shaw, Ian *The Oxford History of Ancient Egypt* (Oxford University Press, 2003)
Shaw, Ian and Nicholson, Paul *British Museum Dictionary of Ancient Egypt* (British Museum Press, 1995)
Siliotti, Alberto *Egypt: Splendours of an Ancient Civilisation* (Thames & Hudson, 2005)
Tyldesley, Joyce A. *Ramesses: Egypt's Greatest Pharaoh* (Penguin Books 2001)
Tyldesley, Joyce A. *Egypt: How a Lost Civilization was Rediscovered* (BBC Books, 2005
West, John Anthony *Serpent in the Sky: High Wisdom of Ancient Egypt* (Quest Books USA, 1996)

Websites

A plethora of information on Ancient Egypt exists on the internet, but be wary of taking everything for fact. However, you may find the following websites of interest:

www.bergen.org/AAST/Projects/Egypt
(Looks at religion, social and cultural life, hieroglyphics, and art.)

www.en.wikipedia.org/wiki/History_of_ancient_Egypt
(History, Art, Medicine, Mathematics, Religion etc.)

www.mnsu.edu/emuseum/prehistory/egypt
(An exhibit in the MSU EMuseum which has information on the culture of ancient Egypt. This site includes information on architecture, art, hieroglyphics etc.)

www.seas.upenn.edu/~ahm/
(Ancient Egyptian Women: Status and Rights, Medicine and Mummification, Mathematics, Art, The *Book of the Dead*, Treasures of the Egyptian Museum, Egyptian Monuments etc.)

www.watson.org/~leigh/egypt.html
(History, Gods and Goddesses, Mythology, Hieroglyphs)

Index